girlie antics
& other shenanigans

by patty clark

Aionios
Books

Damsel in dis Mess: Girlie Antics and Other Shenanigans

Copyright © 2016 by Patty Clark

All rights reserved. This book or parts thereof may not be reproduced in any form, stored in a retrieval system, or transmitted in any form by any means—electronic, mechanical, photocopy, recording, or otherwise—without prior written permission of the publisher, except as provided by United States copyright law.

Cover and title page design: Joey Seward
Photo credits: Lindsay Busca

Version 001
ISBN-13: 978-0-9980844-1-1 (Paperback)

Published by Aionios Books
Carlsbad, California
www.aioniosbooks.com

Praise for the Damsel

♥

"You are going to enjoy this collection of Patty Clark's columns. Her humorous stream-of-consciousness style on down-to-earth, everyday topics will remind you of the late Erma Bombeck, if you're old enough to remember her. I would recommend this book to anyone who would like to add a little humor, mixed with just enough reality to create a unique perspective on life in suburban America at the beginning of the 21st Century."
—Peter J. Cook, Publisher of *The Parson's Sun* newspaper, Kansas

"Not since the days of Erma Bombeck have I read and enjoyed such witty and self-deprecating prose. If she was still around today, Patty would be giving Ms. Bombeck a real run for her money and column space. Patty's columns are always warmly anticipated and received because everyone can use a little levity in their lives. Go Patty!"
—Joe Moris, Peace Columnist for the *Coast News*, Encinitas, California

"In Patty Clark's collection of short stories, I am delighted to find validation for my own experiences. Not enough words can express her clever delivery of the human experience. These stories left me with a wonderful sense of freedom that one is not alone or completely crazy. What you can rely on in her work is the entertainment value coupled with all the thoughts and emotions we all feel but may have never allowed ourselves to express. She takes ordinary experiences to a higher level of awareness, which not only amuses but is

also thought-provoking with a twist of intellectual humor. Each one of Patty's stories moves the reader through such an entertaining and engaging experience that only leaves one grasping for more."
—Penny Rothschild, Owner/Curator, Emerald C Gallery and Ruby P Gallery, Coronado, California

"I have been a follower of Patty's writing for years. Over time, I have seen her humor sharpen, her prose become sleeker, her voice unique and deeply personal. And she's truly a pleasure to read."
—Marta Chausee, Author of *Murder's Last Resort*

"There's an old saying: "When life gives you lemons, make some lemonade." Patty Clark does make lemonade, but she goes the extra step of letting it ferment into 80-proof fun. She transforms everyday vicissitudes into missiles of dissimilar similes and relevant irreverence. The eternal battle between body parts and gravity (spoiler, gravity is winning); the heroic beau who leaves a trail of unwashed socks and offsprings' slings and arrows—they're all in her offering some good snarky-humor fun."
—Russell Shor, Gemological Institute of America, Inc.

"In this hilarious book, Patty shares stories that only a few brave souls would have the guts to tell. She does it with ease because she walks her talk and is the real deal. Get ready to laugh and cry!"
—Katana Abbott, CFP, Life and Legacy Coach and Host of *Smart Women Talk Radio*

"As for that Damsel in dis Mess thing... Patty showed up at our writers' meetup one evening holding a sheaf of paper in one hand and a bottle of merlot in the other.

She introduced herself, and East Hell Writers hasn't been the same since. We are lost when we cannot hear her so-richly crafted humor. After all, we are, through Patty's stories, living her life as well. We also have to put up with pesky skunks, gratuitous bonding experiences, and plumped-up pyromaniacs. You, the reader, will find curiously soothing and jarring parallels to absolutely everything that is within your daily meanderings. There ain't no stress in dis mess."
—Ed Coonce, Oceanside Cultural Arts Foundation Board Member, Host of East Hell Writers, and President and Creative Director of Theatre Arts West, Encinitas, California

Contents

Dear Reader, 1
Photo: A sitting duck for microbes, 5
Bonfire of the Insanities, 6
Absurdia, 10
Inside the Authors Studio, 14
Photo: No itsy-bitsy spider, 18
When Nature Calls, 19
Mama Said There'll Be Men Like This, 23
Comedy of Err-Heads, 28
I Yam What I Yam, 32
Why I Never Became a Nun, 36
My Two Dads, 40
The Ulta-Mate Experience, 44
Photo: You're just too good to be true, 48
Sweet Sailing, 49
Faux Pas, 53
Orange Crush, 57
Oldies but Goodies, 61
Rejection, 65
Worth the Wait, 68
Smartypants, 73
Photo: Granddaughter goofiness, 77
Babelicious, 78
Cold Turkey, 82
Nutcracker, 85
Temple of Doom, 89
Oz-Servations, 93
Calls of Duty, 97
Photo: Exfoliation, 101

My Four Hours of Fame, 102
Man Caving, 106
Sh Sh Sh Sh Sh Sh Sugartown, 110
Doctors Do-Little, 114
The Other Woman, 118
I Got the Music in Me, 122
Somewhere in my Wicked Parenting Past, 126
Photo: Wash today, 130
Will Work for Socks, 131
Estrogen-arian Allies, 135
Hello, Anyone Home? 139
Lovin' Spoonfuls, 144
Clear and Present Wager, 148
Planet of the Grapes, 152
Photo: I never show up empty hatted, 156
Brotherly Love, 157
Good Deeds, 161
The Fugitive, 165
Lordess of the Rings, 169
Against One's Will, 173
Love is a Many Censored Thing, 177
Barbies vs. Kens, 180
Parent Trap, 183
Photo: Guess, 187
Artsy Fartsy, 188
Starstruck, 192
Crimes and Missed-Demeanor, 196
Out of the Mouths of Bigger Babes, 201
Bugged, 205
Two Scents Worth, 209
Cautionary Tales, 213
Photo: Worn like sacred badges of honor, 217
When You Wish Upon a Star, 218
It's my Party and I'll Cry if I Need to, 222

Mom Always Liked Me Least, 226
Blah Blah Blah, 230
Patty Melt, 234
Photo: Liberating myself, 238
Cursed, 239
Goddess of Recreation, 243
Now or Never, 247
Acknowledgements, 252
Photo: Dis be my messy desk! 254
About Patty Clark, 255

Dear Reader,

Darwin said, "It is not the strongest species that survive, nor the most intelligent, but the ones most responsive to change." This book is the evolution of my existence, hoping you get a physiological response from the many changes and absurdities that have occurred. I believe that laughter truly is the best remedy and giggling is good for every infraction. It's only when arachnids are invading my space that I have to resort to sadness and violence.

People have called me the writing wizard. I can magically transform six cups of caffeine into crazy satirical sentences. I am always trying to maintain an air of humor about everything and decided that there just isn't enough in this world that makes us smile. I never saw myself becoming a clown or a game show host. But I wanted to contribute something to the world by releasing all that valuable stuff in my head. So I set out to boldly fulfill my lifelong ambition of writing maniacally in pursuit of some global grins. Not really. It has become extremely therapeutic and a wonderful coping mechanism to unleash the messes that living produces. I write humorously because funny is engaging, and because kidnapping people and forcing them to cackle is technically illegal. Insight comes to life when it's told in a captivating way that makes readers stop and say, "I'm not the only one who feels like that."

There have certainly been times when I wasn't smiling, like last night when I did the dishes. It made me happy knowing my kitchen was clean until I turned around and saw grimy pans still sitting on the stove. But I kept smiling, after focusing on the fact that someone is washing dishes at the Golden Langar Community kitchen in India where they feed up to 100,000 daily. That's a lot of dishes. I don't think I ever smiled during my emotionally filled childhood, when washing dishes for nine siblings took away a large chunk of my happiness. I wanted to say goodbye to tiresome grody dishware by flinging them into a tree. I wish I could have made my parents smile more. The only time I saw Mom and Dad beaming from ear to ear was when they went away for a week and left us with Aunt Nancy.

Then I became a parent myself. Moments when I truly loved the people I was living with often turned sour when I didn't see them smiling. Maybe they thought it would cause pudgy cheeks, or they could have been experiencing a wedgie. I kept getting those neutral expressions similar to indignant serial killers. There were so many times I wanted to tell my kids, "Smile dammit!" Something was blocking their Root Chakras, so I was on a mission to change that. I tried everything from joking and stroking their hair gently, telling them they smell good, to bribing them with cookies. I had to keep reinforcing that they were "pretty pretty pretty pretty pretty pretty girls," while telling myself I was a Beast of Burden. There were times I had to eat the last two cookies knowing I had three children, which made them even more unhappy. Writing kept me from drinking myself into a cosmopolitan coma.

I could have written about how to survive a domestic uprising, or a book about martinis and me. I do have an intoxicating recipe for daiquiri bread. Buy a loaf, pour a daiquiri in a dish, and sop it up with the bread. It has turned some of my frowns into downright joyous occasions where I was able to illustrate events with extra love about those all around me. I began scripting just like Ernest Hemmingway who wrote drunk and edited sober. Although my brain was willing to donate this witty confessional and progression of experiences as a means of therapy that weren't all liquor induced.

Thank God there is coffee, pens, paper, and the computer. At first, I took out every frustration at my desk by playing acupuncture with push pins and pads. I was seconds away from stabbing myself when my first story came to mind. I couldn't get the words out fast enough and yet it was going to take a slew of code-breakers and probably the entire Central Intelligence Agency to interpret what I was trying to convey. Doubt crept in and I wondered if I was really a writer, or a wildly emancipated meerkat with a flair for nonsensical fun. That's when I knew that doodling decapitated stick figures wasn't newsworthy, but writing sentiments about being ready for the sanitarium was. In a short amount of time, I had people writing to me about how relatable my stories were. Thus began my impulsive braggery. Legend has it that nomadic shepherds first noticed the effects of caffeine when their goats danced and appeared wiry after nibbling on coffee beans. My boyfriend has to pour milk on my cereal because I'm too jittery to get it into my bowl. Plus I have way too much on my mind. Any sort of kitchen duty isn't nearly as much fun as scribbling silly stories.

Many things started me on this rant. Mating. Motherhood. Single parenting. Venting proved very profitable and saved me a ton on psychoanalysts. I did read a scientific report on the disturbing subject of non-smilers and wondered, in the event that an earthquake is going to swallow me whole, I'll be glad I illustrated this silly jargon and would like to go out in a smoldering craze of short story. We can all benefit from propositioning ourselves, that both privately and going out in public is met with cheerful enthusiasm for everyone. In saying that, I hope you read this crafty narrative instead of resorting to lavatory walls for entertainment. Mine is the sort of bold and scintillating straightforwardness that comes with being over sixty.

Nothing is going to stop my churning vortex of trivial concerns. This planet is the one place where a person can experience both heaven and hell at the same time. When all is said and done, I obsess over those cherished appendages, my loved ones. So no matter the pokes of fun and frolic, I move rhythmically through the roles of mother, grandmother, mate, friend, sister, and artistic achiever. There are people who build sandcastles. Some jump from planes or rob banks. My joy comes from making comic and creative connections with people in my life and with you, my reader.

Yours forever and ever,

Patty ♥ xxoo

Patty Clark
AKA: Damsel in dis complete and utter mess

Patty Clark 5

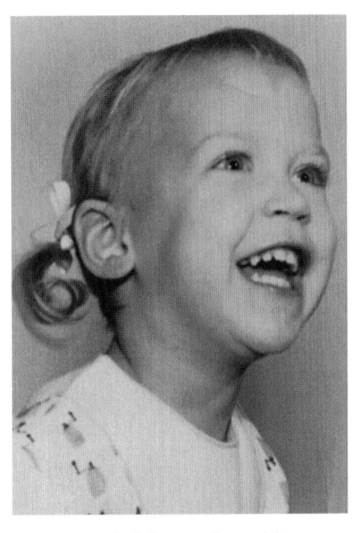

A sitting duck for microbes and future backlashes

Bonfire of the Insanities

Some people would like to torch their insanities and watch them burn. Not me. I enjoy my preposterousness and second childhood. My insanities started at a young age when I was a zit acupuncturist. I learned that there could be adverse effects in the practice of pimple popping that may lead to scarring and possibly go far deeper into the dermis, saturating the very core of my nervous system and damaging my brain. Or at least that's what my brother told me. I wasn't exactly a conformist, but more of a melodramatist and a liberationist. I must have heard my parents say a trillion times, "Have you lost your mind?" My brothers also heard it when they tried to fossilize our pet turtle, and the time one of them decided to be a trapezist by hanging a homemade harness from his bedroom ceiling. I'm sure there's a fine line between insanity and stupidity. None of us thought twice about playing dinner-roll badminton at the dining table, a game that my parents thought was only for anarchists. I myself became a volcanologist when I attempted to cook a whole egg in the microwave, wrapped in aluminum foil. I'm sure I was described as an absurdist. Mom also said I was temperamental. At the time, I wondered if it meant that I was one part temper and most parts mental. Every time I asked for something ridiculous, my parental advisories immediately turned into climatologists when they replied, "Sure. When hell freezes over."

 I hate to admit my shortcomings, but one time when I was a teenager I went out for the evening and came home extremely late. I know it's hard to believe since I was nurtured by nuns and my Dad was only inches away from becoming a priest. I was questioned by my mother the next morning. "Your being late tells me one of three things. You tried running away but got as far as Toledo when you realized you forgot your clothes. Or you stayed somewhere else to watch shows I won't let you watch. Or, you had fallen and could not get up, in which case you should have called me so I could dial 911." Little did I know that I had entered neuroscientific territory when she was identifiably an alarmist. Dad just sat there saying several novenas while Mom was hell bent on interrogating me. It's a good thing she hadn't questioned me the minute I walked through the door or made me walk a straight line. I could have been spewing things unbeknownst to her. Luckily I didn't transform into a redistributionist by barfing up those beers.

Some say illusionists are insane. I guess it depends on what they are imagining. I mean the brain is the most vital organ we have—according to the brain. Was I crazy when I conceptualized my fetuses being boys before birth? It's a wonder I carried my three girls to term when I can't contain a thought for more than two minutes. After bringing my daughters into this screwy world, I taught them to sing. Because they would soon learn that craziness would be crossing their normal brain barriers. But teaching them to be conversationalists eventually backfired on me. They'd whine and complain that I was nagging and suffocating them. I reaped their wrath from many things. Here's one for instance. My daughters wanted to blame me when their girlfriends didn't attend birthday parties at our house because they didn't like my choice of games, such as bobbing for Brussels sprouts. I certainly became a joyist, that emotion elicited by marrying, becoming a mother, divorcing, and raising kids alone. When I could still hear them, I guess I wasn't piling enough sandbags at the base of their bedroom doors. The ancient Babylonians based zodiac signs on behavioral acts. And what we do during pregnancy can determine how a child turns out. Like abstaining from alcohol, tobacco, tuna fish, and sword fighting. I knew that if my newborns came out with any indelible imprints, I'd probably have to spring for reconstructive surgery. Never once did I think about seeing an abortionist. But once or twice I thought of calling an adoptionist. Astrologically speaking, things that happen can have everything to do with the stars being out of alignment.

Everyone is insane to a certain degree. Truth be known, I'm more about being a diffusionist. Yet if someone rides the batty bus or plays out a manic fear of vegetables in the produce aisle or walks around holding a wand professing to be Harry Potter—those things we can only get away with when we're five. Not to label what is insane and what is not, but things I once thought were demented might not be the case now. That random splat of eggs on the microwave walls at the time seemed pretty insane to my mother, who told me I needed my head examined. Today, if someone did that in my microwave, I would call them certifiably silly and you'd hear a resounding laughter coming from my kitchen.

My stouthearted battle of being insane shall continue and I have given in to my inescapable ways of spicing things up. Besides, I have found a simple solution for this. I no longer care what others think of me. But if I ever get beyond the point of no return, hopefully you won't see the madness in my eyes when I'm holding a butcher knife. Even if I were Glen Close who is known for her fatal attraction. I would still have a lot of catching up to do with her. My focus these days is on being a sensationalist, with my subversive imagination and sarcasm. Early on, even though my parents noticed symptoms of cognitive decline, a spoonful of sugar never made the medicine go down. There were so many times they tried talking some sense into me, desperate to save others from my impending silliness. After all, I did wreck the car once and gave my parents shiny fragmented details about what truly happened. But deep inside, I'm a really good person.

Absurdia
♥

I'm not sure which was worse. The buzzing and stinging, or the backlash from neighbors congregating on my lawn while they crushed my finely cultivated greenery.

It all happened one Michigan morning a decade ago when I climbed on my roof to touch up the paint on the garage. And like most masterminds, my work is best done before noon, or during happy hours when I formulate brilliant plans on cocktail napkins. Although the napkins haven't made me a million dollars richer so I can hire people to do these strenuous paint touch ups. My duties are done between five and nine. Am, not pm. I'm pretty much toast after breakfast. So I was on a mission.

I hadn't noticed the nest of wasps hidden in the slat of the louvered window opening. Before long I'm covered with them, and screaming loud enough to wake the people still sleeping in Finland. It did bring my daughter abruptly out of her coma and was heard by my next door neighbor. The concerned and caring person that she was yelled, "Harry, get the can of Raid. There's a wasp on the screen. Then go help the nut next door who has climbed to the peak of her garage and is getting stung by a hundred more."

Two minutes later, my screeches brought a few more neighbors over. All I wanted for Christmas was for my two Freesias to still be standing out front once the bystanders got done pushing them out of proportion. And there was more buzz below me than what was buzzing around me. So much for the focus on moi. The neighbor across the street strongly suggested that my eaves needed painting to enhance my home's value. I never knew he was a home appraiser. I wondered if my swollen hands were able to handle holding the brush a while longer to make his wish come true. My hands would have handled a good punch to his nose. One highness of horticulture told me that my grass needed fertilizing and way better care than what I was providing. Harry, who was holding the can of Raid, wasn't moving quite as swiftly as I hoped. I wanted the slow Secretariat to step it up a bit. But he stood there trying to unclog the spray tip. Another gal yelled up to me, "Did you get your shorts at Target? I almost bought them in blue!" I did wonder what they were all doing at my house when *Regis & Kelly* were on TV. Within five more minutes I had an insatiable longing for solitude, new blue shorts, one of those wasp suits, and flat ground. God didn't have to create numerous kinds of distractions. But unfortunately for me, He did.

People are strange, even when you're not a stranger. One neighbor came over carrying a casserole before I ever got down from the roof. Come to think of it she was dressed in black. Maybe she thought I'd die up there. I know I didn't have a death wish, but I overheard some of the neighbors say I did. If I had suicidal tendencies, I sure wouldn't use my roof for it and leave a huge mess. I would have climbed one of theirs. What was otherwise normal suburbia seemed more like *Disturbia*. Only it was me who wanted to go on a killing spree. But I wouldn't have been content jailed with other weirdos.

Meanwhile I'm still waving away parasitoids like a madwoman. Where was a wasp killing ninja when I needed one? I had my heart set on someone climbing up to help me, but I could see that wasn't going to happen. Then again that person could fall off and sue me. I had this visual of my house being set up like the scene in ET when they finally removed him from the home, and all of us were robed in head-to-toe moon suits. The difference being, I wouldn't cry when the wasps left. I wasn't about to shed tears when the neighbors left either. I remember some faint instruction from my dad who once told me I shouldn't try to balance on steep surfaces unless I liked the idea of free falling and never walking again. Like a dummy, I never listened to my parents. Just about the time I was feeling leery about my chances of survival, I said, "Could someone please hold the ladder while I get down? And I'll gladly pay someone Tuesday for an exterminator today!"

So... how many neighbors does it take to hold a ladder? One couldn't. She was holding the chicken casserole. Harry ended up spraying himself in the eyes with the Raid. The home appraiser was walking around assessing the rest of my property. It was my adoring daughter who came to my rescue after she phoned the fire department.

Once I arrived to safety, I waited for the exterminator, but had to ask if anyone even made that call. From what I experienced, I figured someone would get around to it by spring, 2020. It was just a good thing I wasn't having a baby. One finally arrived and made me spend an extortionate amount of money. Before I paid him, I was uniquely diligent in using bartering as a business arrangement. I tried telling him I'd remove all the bug stains from his outfit with a lifetime guarantee, because it's amazing what a little Oxy and a can of sealer can do to clothing. And when stains don't come out, there's always dying the thing black. An hour into negotiations, I found out how grouchy exterminators can get.

The only way to interrupt the whole absurd neighborhood bonding ceremony was to tell them there was a fire at the Johnson's, or a yard sale at the Dempsey's. When it was time to say good-bye, I don't recall experiencing any separation anxiety. I was just sorry I hadn't contacted Sting to come sing at my wasp wake.

Inside the Authors Studio

The kind of being I normally find attractive depends on my mood. If I'm sitting passively enjoying an episode of *Inside The Actors Studio* with James Lipton, I might be attracted to the type of masculinity who has a love for words. But if I'm interrupted by a terribly eerie home invader, I might be more attracted to a serrated kitchen blade aimed at slaying the aggressor.

It was 2002 and I was a newcomer to southern California. One evening while lounging on my couch playing captive audience to *Actors* interviewee James Gandolfini, I broke out in a stunned condition of watcher's block, prompted by something insidious crawling on my carpeting. The distressing part was that it had already made its way to my dining room which was clear across the room from the open French door where I was sure it came in. I could have previously stepped on it with my bare feet either leaving evil ruins in my carpet fibers, or precipitating all kinds of anger from the stranger. It's too bad I didn't have any fabulous footage of the large eight-legged tarantusaurus that was enjoying my plush lodging and eclectic scenery. I wanted to tell it that I only do tours on Tuesdays, and more precisely with humans. I acknowledged it with a "Heil Hitler" salute, although I would rather Prince Charming showed up on my doorstep, or a Chippendale. I never imagined that one of *Charlotte's Web*-by residents would make itself at home. A thief would have been less creepy than this critter. Trouble soon festers when two opposites find it hard to exist together under one roof.

Meanwhile my cat Stella, who might just as well have answered to Bashful, decided to combat the creature by sitting there silently staring at it. Unlike a dog, who would have bravely gone before me tackling the monster. I could have used a little help with the slaughter, but I suppose my cat didn't want to get her claws dirty or mess up her hair. The beast was having absolutely no luck at all attracting females. I'm a non-violent person, though I'm sure I could respond rather Al Caponishly if I needed to. In retrospect I should have said, "This house is protected by both a security alarm system and a woman in the midst of menopause. Guess which one is far more murderous?"

I tiptoed closer to get a better look at the varmint, staging an ongoing effort to not reveal any hint of my horror. I wanted James Lipton to jump out of the television screen to use his coaxing on the beast since he is very persuasive at getting his guests to provide personal information about themselves. For a minute there, I considered asking the arachnid if I could call a cab for it or inquire how it felt about flesh wounds. But I had more intelligent questions to ask such as: "What is your favorite word?"; "What is your least favorite word?"; "What turns you on?"; "What turns you off?"; and "What profession other than home invader would you like to attempt?" I mean if I was going to have someone in my house, I might as well strike up a stimulating conversation.

During my own interviewing process, the bad brute scurried swiftly out the door like a racehorse suddenly released. I followed it out and found it slithering into a space underneath the threshold. I thought to myself, "Oh goodie. I get to see it again sometime." The next day I described the entity to a co-worker who said,

"Sounds like a tarantula." I went out and bought a sonic plug-in for keeping arachnids away, and I hadn't seen hide nor hair of it since.

My distress did not stop there. Arachnids have cousins. On another occasion, I was sitting in bed when I caught a glimpse of a ginormous web outside the door that held another sickening spider. Only this time it was a black widow, sending me into arachnophylactic shock. Who was I to criticize its silk spinning creativity. Yet I did a month's worth of cardio by grabbing a can of insecticide and a broom in an all out attempt to destroy it. I thought of calling someone for help who was only a 911 phone call or bloodcurdling scream away. Normally, dog-sized daddy long legs never bother me. But with other spiders, I snatch a wad of tissues and very carefully smash it, then proceed to torch it, lighting me and most of my immediate surroundings. It is hardly effective though when a beast is in the bathroom bum tank swimming for safety and I'm yelling, "Fire in the toilet bowl!"

God's garden-ian angels somehow turn into gardenian devils. The insecticide and broom clubbing scenario proved useless. The web shriveled, and the spider escaped. I came home after work the next day and the web had been re-woven with more extensive exoskeletons of doom. The pest must have been offended by my assassination attempt. I needed to do whatever it took to stay safe from conscientious harvestmen, short of building a Berlin-type wall with barbed wire and topped with atomic warheads. To think that the unaccountable coterie of sinister spiders might be inseminating each other and I could have more visitors in my cupboards and closets. I was going to kill this thing before cobwebs began covering me in my sleep.

I heard that the venom from the Brazilian banana spider causes erections in male victims. Being a female, those spiders would certainly be in the wrong place if they wanted to stiffen a guy. What else can I say about tarantulas. Goliath abdomens, fast legs, only slows down with Prozac or a lethal hammer punch to the cephalothorax. Sledgehammering a spider is definitely worth losing fourteen feet of stucco. Journaling my misadventures, I could have concluded these visits by submitting one final question to the intruders. "If heaven exists, what would you like to hear God say when you arrive four feet under?"

This ain't no itsy-bitsy spider!

When Nature Calls

I normally do one important thing when I get out of bed each morning. And it sure isn't lifting weights to tone my triceps. That comes after my morning java eye opener. Only I use soup cans as weights. Empty ones.
There is never a good time to replace that dud toilet. Especially when you are rooming with the homeowner who has a bathroom attached to his master suite that is unavailable to anyone other than his significant other. And you are using the hall bathroom that decided to take a leak leaving standing water, which resulted in the toilet being removed until a decision is made on which plumber can fix it at the right price. I heard quote after quote after quote. At those rates, I thought it would never get fixed. Which brings me to my bulging bladder.
I was out one night, and came home to my roomie already sound asleep. I wasn't exactly doing a happy dance after hearing Zzzz's from behind his closed door. I was forced to piddle outside in the shrubs, something I hadn't done since I was six. Okay, that camping trip was an exception. So was the time I couldn't wait for those gals to hurry up in the restroom at O'Reilly's where I once again had to go outside to bare my behind to a bush. You'd think places would provide America's tax payers top quality service by adding a few dozen more commodes to their establishments, creating integrity and fairness to all.
The next morning I woke, wanting to do what I do every single morning of my life. I began to look as though I was about to have a seizure, moving around

like an over filled water bed. I'm surprised I didn't let the river flow and wet myself right then and there. And I found that trying to relieve the agony by putting pressure on my bladder only put more pressure on my bladder. So I bonded with the great outdoors once more by watering the pachysandra. I didn't want to rain on anyone's parade. Especially if I saw processionary caterpillars in search of soft soil so they can form their cocoons. I had softened the soil enough to be able to dig to China rather easily.

Now you know what happens right after that first cup of coffee. Sipping a hot brew is often accompanied by a gastrointestinal effect when the colon decides to perform one of its key functions. And too much witholdin' can create an itty bitty bit of a tummy ache. I highly doubted that any ground crawling critters wanted to see my bum again. Nor was I about to set that good example to anyone in the entire insect kingdom. I just hoped I wouldn't be seeing myself peeing in some near future remake of Candid Camera or on YouTube. I heard that four out of five people suffer from paruresis, the inability to pee in the presence of others. So I guess the fifth person must enjoy it. Although it's really not my kind of fun. But what choice did I have, other than become a frequent restroom attendee at the corner gas station.

Thomas Jefferson said, "It is neither wealth nor splendor; but tranquility and occupation which give you happiness." Well, I'd have a whole lot of tranquility if I could use a real restroom when I needed to. Plus, happiness would surround me more if I never had to work again. And if those who do work, like plumbers, would just show up instantly when called to do their job, I wouldn't have to strike up conversations with grasshoppers. Then again, the insects could gather round while I do a splendid Ricky Nelson rendition of *Garden Party*, because I would be reminiscing with old friends who all know my name but may ask me to stay seated throughout my entire performance. They could certainly catch me before I embarrass them or myself if I walk away with toilet paper dangling from my backside. It's more likely I'd hear one of them singing "Hot diggity, dog ziggity, boom what you do to me!"

That was Tuesday and still no plumber within fixing distance. The weekend came, and no one likes working on weekends. Except maybe contractors who charge double time and want you to throw in a twelve pack and some sub sandwiches. Then basically they botch the job and you end up calling someone else on Monday. By then it's Tuesday again, one week later with no end in sight other than my own.

I like to think I'm a responsible irrigator. When the subject of sanitation is in question, I'm not the only one with an indecent disposal. Dogs do it. Cows do it. So no one should taboo the topic of tinkling when the ends justify the means of making good compost in places that don't have privacy doors attached to them. I came up with Plan B, which was knocking on the neighbor's door at six in the morning to borrow their bathroom. They weren't nearly as pleasant as the first five times I asked. I was doing better with Plan A, or using the service station restroom. They don't call it service for nothing. I'm sure the attendant there was elated to see someone stroll in, interrupting his newspaper reading ritual to witness a woman in moose slippers and no make-up, still lathered in nighttime rejuvenation cream.

All this taught me to arm myself with more absorbent tissues to avoid lingering longer in the nether regions of nature. And fanny bug bites gave me incentive to move. So I got a place of my own where plumbing problems are dealt with more promptly. I thought of residing in a high rise. But if it ever happened again, I might not make it quick enough to ground level.

Mama Said There'll Be Men Like This

Snow White could have settled for all seven dwarfs. But she may not have wanted to escort a band of small people. It seems like they would have been a whole lot of fun with the exception of Grumpy, that naysayer with the disposition of a cactus and very similar to some of the dates I've encountered. I'd rather hang out in a leper colony or sequester myself in Asia wading with water buffalo.

My first introduction to the male anatomy was not at home around a father and six brothers. We were vacationing at my godfather's cottage on the Canadian seaboard one summer weekend when I caught a glimpse of him in the wee hours walking through the hall with his robe open and flesh-like thingy protruding. I didn't want to forfeit a rare chance to bond with the man who at one time coochie-cooed me and carefully held me over a baptismal basin. But I was very young and impressionable at this sudden circumspection. Plus, I was too shy to ask if he was sleepwalking, or if the dog chewed his bathrobe belt. Besides, he was too consumed with the timely task of groping himself. It was more than I expected in terms of hospitality. Good thing it was warm outside or I may have worried his tenderloins would get frost nipped. It was that very moment when my assumption of older men was compiled in one word. Icky.

Time went on. I entered the dating scene and learned more about the male psyche. One guy in high school peaked the beefcake category until this Don Juan of a date drove me through a car wash thinking it would be comical to roll down the windows on my side of the car. The laughing hyena watched as the sudsy power wash switched to dry, pressure pulling my skin nearly off my drenched body. I kept thinking if this was his way of winning me over, I'd get more joy out of going over Niagra Falls in a barrel, by myself. There are infinitely better ways to humor me. Going to a male model academy doesn't make anyone handsome any more than buying a Powerball ticket will make someone rich. Mama did tell me that if I wanted some spice in my life, to marry a man who uses tarragon, and could make me laugh. But Dom DeLuise had already been taken. I also made my pitch to Sean Connery, but some women snag these men up faster than those running for the food vendors at Costco.

Eventually I married, and it faded like steam on a mirror. I didn't expect total bliss, but I did expect that a life sentence of unity would be somewhat in sync. I figured someday I would find the right guy. I always consider not sailing into very deep water without knowing how my odds would play out during shark season, if you know what I mean. Tom Petty has given great emphasis to the fact that if you listen to your heart, it's going to tell you what to do. Well, it didn't tell me anything when I dated the smothers brothers, Tyrannosaurus Rex, and those men who were desperately seeking Suzanne, Marsha, Jane, or anyone else carrying chesticles. I guess I could simply stay home and watch my gray hairs progressing. A single male friend said he's gone out with Cruella and all sides of Sybil. So women aren't exempt as bad dates. Unpleasurable escorts played out with increased frequency and I figured if I can't be with the one I love, then I can love the one I'm with as

long as he has a stash of good chocolate.
As luck would have it, I prepped for another night of enamoring. I showed up that evening like a charged battery with only a twinge of trepidation. Awaiting me was somebody's father's grandfather with dentures and a tipped toupee, who looked to be about a hundred and four. He was however breathing on his own. I was feeling particularly pretty too because I brushed my teeth and everything. I could have probably followed him home if I was into playing Canasta for ten torturesome hours. Talk about your buzz kill. Prince Charming turned into prince alarming. I wasn't sure which of us was going to need a mobile medical unit first. I wanted to bolt over the threshold and flee immediately. Transforming into Road Runner would have tickled my funny bone once more. But I stayed long enough to enjoy a Merlot while he enjoyed his Metamucil mixed with cranberry juice. I wanted to harangue the gal who hooked me up with this man. Boy, did I ever get the ol' switcheroo. I thought it was going to be her cute and charming Sam from her hiking group. Not senile Sam from the old folk's home. I was never great at differentiating between middle-aged voices or old. Telling me he liked naps should have been a dead giveaway.

My girlfriends and I commiserrate over the pipsqueaks and piranhas and whether to put up with the absurdities of bar scenes. But the need to unwind beckons us. We certainly have enough stories to share about dating deviates, and try to stay open minded when bitten by the bug of a bad one. There were times I felt sixteen again with my party dress and goose bumps awaiting a date. Others end up as thrilling as free falling bare naked from a plane in a Fargo deep freeze. Some have duped me after expecting a younger model, when they weren't patient enough to contently tolerate these defined qualities within me. I can get my groove on. Just not in a tube top with my stomach showing. Other men look at me as if I'm a mouth watering triple cheeseburger. Depending on who is standing next to us in a drinking establishment, we are either savoring our liquid libations or fighting off bugging barflies with an urgency to guzzle and skedaddle. One male became quite obtrusive and obnoxious. And although I was cherishing the depths of his adoring dimples, I was also taken back by his shallowness and antagonism. He shared with us his well earned and deserved documentation commemorating his right to administer anesthesia. But Mr. Romanceologist didn't have a license to be a boor. I speculated guys like that needed their own physicians for purposes of ruptured egos. He informed us that he had a hundred friends on Facebook, ninety-six still pending. It's not exactly enchanting standing at arm's length with someone who is going into the third act of Snorkel Bob while goosing my girlfriend. My friend did tell Sir Galahad that his lordship texted wanting him to return to Camelot.

I've had other pangs of disappointment when a blind date I hoped was the facsimile of Jason Statham bore more resemblance to Tiny Tim. It turned into a romantic comedy when he threw cash down on the restaurant table after dinner and mentioned a motel. That didn't alarm me as much as the pictures of his pet snake. And although going home with him certainly seemed like a fantastic offer, I wanted to end that date with "please lose my number." I have, however, had some very enchanted evenings with guys who can crack me up and dunk me on a dance floor. A man can bring me dozens of roses, be a humanitarian, good Samaritan, organ donor, and penthouse owner, and still be Mr. Wrong. But they are certainly wonderful attributes to be adorned with.

Back to those dwarfs. Maybe someday I'll find Aimful, Cheerful, Masterful, Peaceful, Artful, Blissful, or my real match, Kooky.

Comedy of Err-Heads

If somebody has to look up the definition of an airhead, it means they may be one. It also means someone's head is likely full of empty space. To clarify though, three airheads together could mean something entirely different. Like just the lack of being educated in well, most newer things. One of which is technology.

So this blonde, brunette, and redheaded medley of brainiacs were together one day at the brunette's condo. It has an underground garage in which you need both a key to get into or the car remote, and a key to the elevator to get to the third floor condo. We were, I mean they were, congregated in the condo ready to drive the blonde home. The brunette had her five-month-old granddaughter with her, because her visiting daughter and son-in-law needed some alone time. But they weren't alone long after leaving their child in the care of female clones Larry, Moe, and Curly.

The three stooges grabbed the car seat and headed down to the garage, because any highway regulated authorities will tell you that you have to buckle kids in for safety. And not many successes are achieved in such endeavors without the likes of three, mind you, rather intelligent human beings. A half hour later we still, I mean they, didn't have the baby seat securely fastened into the vehicle. Apparently you need to turn the traveler around in the other direction for the safety belt to wrap through indentations specifically manufactured for said strap, which affixes the whole apparatus properly. What's more, you need to be fully informed how the actual seat clamps into the base of the contraption. The three women who had children once themselves never did get it right. But in our...excuse me, their defense, it was a dark and dimly lit garage. Which totally made the redhead want to contact the architect to ask him what he was thinking while designing a garage that would eventually retain silly people who need glasses to see anything, let alone try to see in the dark. And it was a pitch-black colored seat to boot. Plus, the actual car had an ebony colored interior. Not neon yellow. Or at least tan, so they could see things a bit better.

The redhead was holding the baby in one hand and talking on her mobile phone with the other, while the brunette's cell went off underneath the diaper bag inside the car. The brunette began drilling the redhead with directives to quickly find the dang thing. It was like a horse trainer rearing a stallion. So the woman holding the baby and her own cell phone began a desperate attempt to search for the ringing gizmo. Meanwhile the blonde, who was inside the vehicle, was borderline blasphemous. She started pulling the seatbelt practically out of its socket to get it to fit all the way around the blasted baby holder. And obviously the baby was still a couple years away from talking and educating them. The women's discomposure resulted in the garage bulging with echoing sentiments I'll not mention. There may have even been a little panty leakage. And I'm not talking from overhead pipes in a parking structure. None of them could contain themselves long enough to stop the drainage. Why suffer from stupidity when you can enjoy every second of it?

The brunette's daughter caught up with us, I mean them, before the accomplices began their transiting...

taking the baby back for the child's health and well being. I guess taking the tot out again was purely provisional unless the brunette stuck within all the guidelines of general baby care. The farcical threesome proceeded, stopping at the grocers for a few items. Forty-five minutes and two cartfuls later, the car was brimming with three middle aged babes and their bags. After dropping off the blonde, the brunette and redhead ventured back to the condo and entered the garage, or what was originally known as comedy central. Or the scene of the car seat crime, whichever way you want to look at it. They got to the elevator and the brunette announced that she had given the key to her daughter. Another forgetful female approached asking if we had a key to get in because she left hers somewhere. She called her hubby to come let everyone in. While waiting, the blonde called asking the brunette to look in her car for the bottle of rum she had left behind. The brunette walked all the way back to her automobile and found nothing. The blonde called back again confessing that she had never purchased the bottle at the store in the first place. As she ultimately recalled, the cashier never rang her up. This of course concludes that all the hair bleaching did not completely circumvent her brain. And obviously she hadn't yet consumed the alcohol, which could have been more motivation for mindlessness. It must be the same way you feel when the air is sucked out of a blowup mattress. Which is assuming you are a mattress.

After being liberated from that disruption, the brunette's daughter subjected them to a half-hour seminar on how to basically work a baby seat, which was all the brunette and redhead could have wished and prayed for. But by that time, they were unequivocally exhausted. So

the redhead decided it was time to leave them to their own devices.
I have summarized one thing. You should not have these three women together, let alone one by herself, trying to figure out modern mechanics. Women over the age of thirteen are just dense depositories for repeated badgering. And for maximum effectiveness, a lap harness pulled completely out of its retractor (broken) can only hold a very large occupant when it comes to fast acceleration and strong deceleration during transportation. It is how one must feel when riding a roller coaster, or a jetting sports car. At least with the brunettes I know anyway.

I Yam What I Yam

In high school, I wanted to be just like Ann. I loved the way she looked, how she charmed, and innocuously lured all the boys to her yard. Ann, however, wanted to be like Lynn. There was something about Lynn's charisma that intrigued her. Lynn, on the other hand, was impressed with Jennifer. But Jennifer had a hero as well. She wanted to be like me. Turns out, all I had to do was be myself. Yet a girl had to wonder. If human cells are replaced every seven years, I never knew who the heck I was going to be.

Growing up, I spent a lot of flourishing identity time idolizing famous women. Agatha Christie. Farrah Fawcett. Betty White. Betty is splendidly humorous. Farrah had a hot bod and great hair. And Agatha could write. But the teen years yielded unidentifiable results. I was forever trying to find myself, sometimes behind the locked bathroom door facing my reflection. "Mirror, mirror on the wall" was my standard questioning while my siblings stood outside practically wetting their pants. But dad said that port-a-potties would just depreciate the property value. Thankfully the time spent evaluating my entity wasn't caught on some hidden camera. People wonder when I began talking to myself. I was about three when I started all those facial aerobics. I should have been either a physiognomy contortionist or a cartoonist.

I wasn't an exclusive arbiter of mirror watching. My girlfriends did the same thing. One day a playmate decided she wanted to be me and I agreed to be her. So we took on the devilish act of disappearance, with both our parents being completely incognizant of our switching places. I pulled it off by blending nicely into her brood of eight. She, on the other hand, came running back to her house yelling at me for not doing my homework or cleaning my room and demanded that we change places again immediately. So much for a shared friendship. If she had been a devout replacement, she would have picked up my clothes and solved those hard trigonometry problems for me.

Hanging out at her home was no different than being at my house with my own renegade brothers. One minute her male siblings were terrorizing me with worms and, the next, calling me chicken for not daring to jump off their roof. I didn't know if I was fish or fowl. It was a clear case of mistaken identity confusion and I found myself sticking my tongue out and yelling to those rascals, "I know you are, but who am I?" I knew who they were. I narrowed the list down to a pack of halfwit hotshots. I had this nutty theory that in the course of this adventure, their mother would slap them upside the head. But she was used to having rapscallions. She also never bothered to look at faces at her dinner table. Assuming I was her daughter, she asked when I dyed my hair blonde and started biting my fingernails.

If you had asked the boys in school what they found beautiful about me, the dedicated voyeurs would have said my breasts. Even so, mine didn't look as good as Deborah's. Not everything in life is framed by beautifully rounded hydrangeas, so I had to light up lives with an eclectic bevy of other characteristics. Long nails didn't define me unless I was prepared to date Edward Scissorhands. I tried plumping my hair to look like Farrah's. But without the styling help of hair professional

Jose Eber, my mane always appeared as if there was no gravity.

It was bad enough I couldn't find myself behind the massive amount of metal in my mouth. But I found that I could generate attention through some awfully luscious lip gloss with two simple ingredients. Vaseline and peach pulp. Inner beauty is great, but I figured a little mouth seductiveness just might bring all the boys to my yard instead of Ann's. Yet I learned from experience that long hair and a pound of lip gloss was a struggling combination in a wind, or when fans were blowing. So was my mother and any boy who came near me. She was always the abrupt reminder that sex was to remain precious, and never performed on her premises. But like any girl, I was curious. My parents did catch me getting ready to go out in outfits that didn't befit my innocence. They told me the less I encouraged provoking male libidos, the better. They wanted me to be a nun, and must have thought we were the Von Trapp family when I overheard them saying, "How do we solve a problem like Maria." I knew darn well they were referring to me. I suppose I could have gone on to make an expensive hourly wage as a floozy. But I was the least of their worries once the rest of my siblings entered the world and fraught them with difficulties. I think I turned out okay considering I'm prayerful and drink alkaline water daily to stay as pure as possible.

No one ever knew exactly who I was on a resume either. I was an overachiever with a boat load of inaccuracies that made me look stupendous. I may not have looked great in person, but I looked ridiculously good on paper. Most of the time my name was Patty, but on occasion Pinocchio, with a slight variation on the nose. I kept being congratulated for having been head of the class and homecoming queen four times. After toiling tremendously with an identity crisis, now I know exactly who I am. I'm the queen of Home Goods spending, a real hell on heels, but more of a cursive and often cursing post-traumatic parochial attendee with the gift of gab and a blood flow of vintage grapes. I'm also intelligent enough to figure out that one and one is two, in a crisis any wine will do, and if I could just find the right hairdo, I would feel thoroughly complete...and what a wonderful world it would be.

Why I Never Became a Nun

I can equate my high school captivity with baseball. Or at least one year of it. With an all male school situated right next door to our female academy, we were restricted in commingling with players of the "other team." It was my freshman year, and we were constantly benched with a bunch of ground rules and no outs. There were no boys permitted and certainly no DNA left on any school surfaces, since the nuns used their own CSI committee of internal inspectors to constantly scour the landscape for anything male related. My body, which only belonged to the cloistered members of apostolic celibacy, was not authorized to go to first base.

The holy creatures of habit put the fear of God in me. But there were some girls who started certain mating rituals the minute they were in the presence of young fastballs. Which I called entering the big leagues. That sort of scoring position resulted in being immediately extradited to some far away house of shame. Then came nine months of obstetrician visits, a bloody delivery, and eighteen years of extensive child care. I had already listened to babies screaming for eighteen straight years of my life at home plate. I wasn't about to repeat that not-so-peaceful experience so soon. Statistics in my household showed that pregnancy didn't drop off significantly until my mother was well over thirty-seven, which left solid evidence that she was never nurtured by nuns. Baby making was the farthest thing from my plans for contact play. In the back of my mind, I did wonder how ballplayers dealt with increased penetration of the media when batters rose in popularity. I also wondered how you solved the problem of pregnancy. I assumed shackles, or a real good swing and a prayer.

None of the girls I knew went away to such a place, unless they haven't told me yet. With the entire boy's school reeking of Old Spice, I'm sure they hoped the scent would slowly wind its way through our open windows. The mere smell of a guy sent the girlish student body into a total frenzy. Suffering through our separation status with such male dominance so close by made us base our entire social calendar around them. But the more restrictions we had, the more my refined and ever so proper daily living resembled a prison camp. Especially since good ol' boy Phil Richardson walked around with a persistent pucker, and I couldn't take him up on his offer to swap saliva, let alone get close enough to even pucker back. I wasn't used to anyone more x-rated than Opie Taylor or Lassie. The closest I got to true love was when Jack McNeely placed himself in a fielding position and tried to convey how much he liked me. But both the poor guy's stuttering plus Mother Superior stood as interference. It totally impeded any progress of advancement on our playing field. Once the Motherload, I mean Sister, forced me back to class, I figured she was giving Jack lessons in manhood by becoming a designated hitter.

I really wanted Brian Jenkins to like me. Only he didn't either due to my bashfulness, or my cheeks which were covered with an array of acne. And of course the nuns, who wanted to subdue me with teargas. I was treated like Ayatollah Khomeini since they threatened me to a life in exile if I even treaded on male turf. Women of the convent were shrewd, simply shrewd. I didn't need to follow the angelic nunsense of these women. There was no trying to talk me into a life as a heat stroke victim inside layers of heavily robed religious wear. I would have been more in favor of a simple business suit. Besides, nuns never took my humor in the playful spirit in which it was intended. It was bad enough that the little trouble I did evoke resulted in me saying the rosary well into the night. Word had it that one of the boys confessed to his impure thoughts and was asked by the Monsignor, "Are you still entertaining those impure thoughts?" The boy responded, "No. I usually let those thoughts entertain me!" For every seasoned pro who ever felt the sting of a ruler, I know now why they call them rookies.

I never want to balk at those who dedicate themselves to serving the Lord. But after one year of quiet reflection into the extolled virtues of my sex-less girls' school duration, I begged my parents into letting me go to the public school. And in a momentary loss of their right minds, they let me go. I still considered myself a good roamin' Catholic, even if I did have a slight reaction to all things uniformed. At least at the public school I was able to carry on a conversation eye to eye with a guy. Although I must say, the nuns did teach me virtues. But if men smell of Old Spice, I'm probably going to follow them anywhere. I will continue to be reverent when it comes to dressing like a nun at Halloween or putting out "Ale Mary" napkins at my parties. Plus, my perseverance won't cease when inviting friends over with benefits, those benefits of bringing the beer of course because it's their moral obligation. Except that I'm much more accustomed to having bread and wine.

The one disturbing difference between baseball and Catholicism is that I couldn't eat a hot dog if it was Friday or I would end up in Hell instead of Tiger Stadium. Let me tell you, it's been a lifelong struggle avoiding sin. But I believe I am now a product of the old school system since I pray before every exam at the DMV, genuflect before entering baseball bleachers, and refrain from swearing loudly when my team is losing.

My Two Dads

So often I look to my fathers. There was a period when I only acknowledged one of them. It was the man who conceived me, fed me, clothed me, and swore under his breath at me throughout my teens. When I took off that one time, (who said I ran away?) my poor paternal provider hunted me down like a bloodhound. I'm sure my Godly Father had his eyes on me the whole time. And for the couple hours I skipped school, I hoped I would get kicked out so I could enjoy the rest of that day. I'm not sure why my absenteeism was such a sin. It was just one less person to reprimand.

Both dads created me. But only one tried to mold me, scold me, then crucify me for not obeying curfews or for putting marshmallows on random car antennas. My moral compass kept misdirecting me. I am positive the day will come when we are all united together addressing all the dastardly deeds I did during my upbringing as I held the hand grenade to disasters. I didn't mean to offend, repeatedly. Just as dogs messes are an ongoing embarrassment to their owners, I too was forbidden to defecate on neighboring lawns or eat slobberingly at the dinner table. I suppose I should be grateful I was never leashed to a tree. It was always annoying being scolded. Especially by peers so versed in repetitive lessons that I failed to grasp any masterful advice. And with a gut made of guilt, I worried that the heavenly hierarchy would strike me down in order to wake me up. I stopped wearing wild colored clothing so it wouldn't be that easy to pick me out of a crowd.

I had it tough. I was too young to drive or drink. Too young to vote or slip out of the house every so often without adult supervision. I stood strong in these faces of opposition and rebelled against both dads. I realize now that it's a risky position for a parent when a kid shows repugnance. Earth dad kept raising the bar, by using tumblers for his martinis instead of regular glasses. Diety Dad just punished me by not giving me things I prayed for, like a tree house. In Yosemite.

I thought it was God who said, "Go forth and conquer." So I did. I tried to take control of every situation and get the better of the mighty poobah who shared my house with me. Then I found out it was King Arthur who made that statement. Our heavenly Father really said, "Go forth and sin no more." It's taken me awhile to perfect that one. I would probably have fewer regrets on my deathbed had I not been so troublesome. I thought that wearing a fig leaf to the block party would symbolize my alliance towards both fathers. Not according to mom. She sent me home to change because dad was hiding behind a tree not wanting to confirm any association with me.

It was during my growing spiritual awareness that I finally discovered Sam's Club isn't the only saving place. I started pivoting between my two makers and am obligingly thankful now for much of their interrogation and intervention. Strangely, I can still see them both pointing their fingers at me from afar. Since my slight transformation into an earth angel, I am trying to reshape my head to fit into a halo. With my higher Father hovering over me, there's no telling what may happen. He could grab that halo at any moment and give it to someone else. I just hope He doesn't hang it over that woman who forged her way in front of me at

Walgreen's.

I've had a great many conversations with the Man Unseen, and the man I see on occasion in Florida. I've never asked my bigger Daddy if He likes to golf or fly fish up there. I'll bet a cloud would be a more cushy place to sit while waiting for bass to bite. But it would take a real miracle to get a hole-in-one from the sky. There are so many unanswered questions. It's nice having men in my life who can answer me or snap their fingers to make things right. Except, I'm curious. What if God is a woman? And what if Her answers are completely different from a man's? There are other questions besides. I want to ask my predecessor, "So when was the moment you determined that having ten children was a fabulous idea?" I'm sure his reasoning meshed ideally with my desire to wash a dozen dishes instead of just two or three. And here is a question for the bigger Guy. "What was Noah thinking when he allowed those two bees on board?"

I was taught to be a Good Samaritan and spread the Word. Good deeds never go unpunished. Or so I've heard. One day I was returning home from the market and stopped at a street light. A homeless guy approached holding a can. I looked in my wallet. All I had was a twenty. I scoured my purse for change. I couldn't give him my free car wash card. Or my shoes, since I was a size eight and he was undoubtedly a size ten. I reached into my grocery bag for the pound of peanuts. By then, he had walked four car lengths behind me grabbing someone else's money, probably accepting a twenty dollar bill. A policeman came and gave me a citation for holding up traffic. I gave him the peanuts and began to spread these Godly words... "Here, now go forth and give those out to all the people on the streets instead of tickets."

I lied about the fig leaf. But I figured if I wasn't hurting anyone, both my dads would be okay with it. My wingspan is still growing.

The Ulta-Mate Experience

Women know that however bad life gets, all they have to do is go anywhere that sells clothes or beauty products and they can go home feeling far better. I wasn't depressed, just on a mission to replace my discontinued lipstick. And without being disparaging, I entered a store that starts with U and ends with A. Now normally when I enter a cosmetic store, I can hardly get anyone to wait on me. I swear they hide out in back rooms or go for extra long coffee or cocktail breaks. Or maybe they use the old "my grandmother is dying" excuse and fly off to New York for lunch. All I know is that these places have become as popular as pharmaceutical and liquor emporiums and they should have plenty of people who can willfully wait on you.

On a recent visit, I was atypically and rather gladly greeted by four beauty fanatics who had nothing else to do but decide that my face should be a Henri Matisse painting with lots of color and dimension. I suppose they thought I was the very picture of an ancient traveler of the Wild West who went gallivanting over the countryside by way of a covered wagon without taking proper care of my face. So much for natural beauty. It's not my fault I resemble a pasty and not so pretty blanched vampire. I was never going for the *Twilight* look on purpose. Maybe I was born with it, maybe it's chlorine. City officials should never be putting that chemical in our tap water. I am not going to issue a public apology for the way I look before my morning greasepaint.

Next thing I knew, I was pulled into a beauticians chair as a canvas for eyebrow penciling, lip lining, and cheek contouring. The complete decorating turned me into an instant hooker. You could have called me a covered girl. Easy and sleazy beautiful. All I needed were fishnets, a low cut blouse with a push-up bra, and a twenty-year-old's mid-section. Anyone could see that with mussed up hair and a little help from Victoria's Secret, I would be ready for prime time on any city street corner.

With all the fashionable sketch artists handling me, I needed to remain calm around wands and brushes that could easily poke my eyes out. I'm sure other customers weren't pleased with the acoustical moaning that accompanied my makeover, as if the cosmeticians were reconstructing my face with surgical instruments. And when is a bit of blush too much? When you look like a tomato. The red loving craftswoman said, "Let's take your lashes to luxurious lengths." I wanted to ask if they will get me to a four-hundred-foot yacht in the Mediterranean. Another hovering consultant told me, "My, what beautiful eyes you have," adding, "but my oh my, I can fix those sunken cheekbones." She was a wolf alright. It was enormously flattering. The third sales assistant chimed in, "How about a new lip look." And the fourth gal had to get the last words in: "I'd like you to rethink your nail polish, or lack thereof." Being the truly talented individuals that the fine staff of professionals were, I didn't want them attacking my breasts and making mountains out of my mole hills.

Maybe I misunderstood the geniuses of painted nails in technicolor dream coats, where their every day is devoted to arranging hand takeovers as well. Then my lips became their primary concern. The women looked at me funny and continued to coat my tender mouth rims with every tube tone available. My worries were normally reserved for late night insomnia. But in this case, I was stricken with thoughts of getting some dubious side effects from these tubes, like lip-to-brain damage. There was no end to the wealth of bacteria I could obtain. I'm surprised those lipsticks hadn't been taken away by the Center for Disease Controllers. God knows there are other things that need to touch my lips like kisses and margaritas. I don't want to have to rub noses with a person or a drink. To top things off, the cosmeticians never found me the right shade. Every time they applied a new one, I pointed to an ad where a gal was wearing the color I was looking for and said several times over, "I'd like THAT color." I also had to disregard the unplushness of their facial tissues which could have easily passed for industrial grade sandpaper. I wondered if it was too soon to cancel my ULTA-mate rewards program.

In revitalizing beauty for my aging face, I have to take into wallet-size consideration the price of products so I don't go bankrupt. I may buy a $30 bottle of hair conditioner, but I roll my hair with empty vitamin bottles to avoid purchasing a curling iron. Do you know how many bottles of vitamins I've gone through to do this? Those wellness capsules should keep me healthy into the twenty-sixth century. But I can't give up cosmetics. With all my age spotting marks of maturity, I don't want to play connect the dots if I have too much time on my hands and no makeup.

I analyzed the extent of these cataclysmic changes, and my coverage was eventually cut short, which meant being finally released from the four people who held me hostage. And if it hadn't been for my decision to claim homesickness, I'd still be there. I left the restorative shop to meet a girlfriend for lunch. When she saw me she said, "For the love of God, girl! Unless you want to work with Bozo, you might wanna go easy on the face paint."

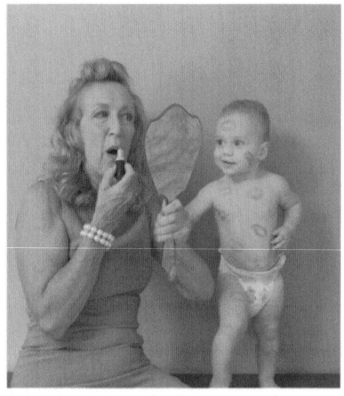

You're just too good to be true; can't keep my lips off of you!

Sweet Sailing

It seems our children are all having children. Assuming they are old enough to remember the wreck of the Edmund Fitzgerald and falling victim to the high waves of a storm, which is very symbolic of parenting. So to all of you setting sail, I hate to be the bearer of bad news. But caretaking comes with some turbulence and the need for a good fitting life jacket. Take it from me—the advanced fetal monitoring system and owner of three fine female vessels.

I wish I could have ruefully studied that entire living arrangement before going through the painful task of labor. What did I know? I figured you have a great time conceiving, go through a few ouches during delivery, hold a cute newborn until they can walk, then set seasonal haul records by chauffeuring till you've spanned the continent. Little was I aware that some scary animals inhabit the waters. And sometimes those animals can bite the very hand that feeds them. Thank the Lord I didn't have boys. Especially if the doctor assesses the baby's private frontal projection area and proclaims, "He's going to be very popular!" Although if you are a seafaring male mollusc, you are only able to copulate once. What a concept. But as I told my fertile mermaids, it only takes once.

I set sail three times, which made it hard to elicit sympathy from other shipwrecked mothers. I got out of my berth every day to the same rituals. Although brushing my teeth never added any splendor to someone actually paying attention to something I had to say. Then came the squabbling. I don't like to be entertained while I'm thinking, just like I don't like to be interrupted while I'm eating. I began suffering something called structural failure. In other words, losing my mind. It got to the point of more frequent inspection of shipmates and their surroundings. There were enough clothes on the floor to outfit the Edmund Fitzgerald's entire crew. And you'd think they wouldn't want to shower in such a yucky rain locker. But asking my girls to clean together was like having orca interact with a great white. Since my girls shared bunks, I wanted to erect barbed wire between their beds to cut short any conspiracies to kill each other. That's when I had more stunning frequencies of unclear thinking. I, the captain, did try keeping a tight ship. It's funny how a swig of straight vodka followed with a Courvoisier chaser seemed to make the madness mellow. Not that I advocate drinking while captaining a ship.

    I traveled through some high velocity winds. It usually meant sparking getaway cancellations, itinerary changes, and our mutt fleeing out the doggie door when the screaming began. I urged anyone else in the path of these storms to take cover. They packed enough of a punch that I felt an evacuation to Tahiti was in order. Hurricane threats stayed in effect for much of my children's remaining years at home. They could have deserted, since some sailors were grumpy over food shortages, meal choices, and curfews. I said, "This isn't the Carnival cruise line!" One day I served them ground beef and told them to throw some BBQ sauce on it and they would think it was ribs. There were times I treated them to steak, knowing full well they would rather take a trip to Taco Bell or the mainland mall with several hundreds of my dollars to blow.

One time the impact of category three winds appeared which typically followed daily boredom or lost sneakers. Minutes after that mood dissipated, sustaining gusts mounted again after one brutal outlash. Sometimes lightening struck, scorching my eyes at the sight of report cards. I declared an emergency, and disaster efforts were called in. With no formal training, I could have issued more storm warnings. I landed in sick bay, visiting many a doctor in those days. Along with my dentist who once told me that I needed a crown. I totally agreed with him that a tiara would suit me nicely.

Any enlightened individual will tell you it's better to have children than not. Of course it's the exhausted commander with stretch marks who will buck that theory. I hate to dissuade anyone from foaling a possible oceanographer, marine architect, or pirate. We all love Captain Jack Sparrow. And if you have Sparrow's state of mind, you may be compelled to try his comedic influence. But I can assure you that you'll need more than that, like degrees in mathematics, mechanics, nursing, technology, superior credentials in communication, and a personal injury lawyer. Not to mention practice aboard another person's ship before sailing out to sea which theoretically, is time aboard a tanker, not a tugboat. And be prepared in case the ship capsizes.

I also recommend cutting coupons for just about everything, if you catch my thrift. In the time it took me to sign up for pre-school, I had already done all the trigonometry, linear algebra, and extended calculus to estimate and allocate future financials. Hopefully there will be some clear skies ahead after your own daughters come to you with shorty shorts, made from the finest scissor cuts in Gap clothing. And I realize it's quite a standard strategy to see boys flinging wee wee over the porch railing that leaves morbid looking marigolds. But I do suggest the little nippers stop breast feeding by the time they grow teeth. Get stern. Boobs are not objects of prolonged production.

At least there is one perk to being predominantly older. My granddaughter wouldn't think of looking at me doltishly. I made all my mistakes with the first two then had a more prosperous voyage with my third. It's much sweeter sailing with grandchildren. My children have all since journeyed into the sunset. Otherwise I would have square knotted my neck to a hull. For the sake of encouraging aspirants navigating a career in child rearing, you could either abstain, or know all the distress signals, plus how to compensate for an enormous amount of motion sickness.

Faux Pas

Ivan the Terrible probably started everything. History presents disparate accounts of his episodic outbreaks. He was, however, a devout leader who was widely popular among commoners. Then there's me. Widely popular among squirrels, since I feed them daily. They have yet to witness my outbreaks. But they don't antagonize me. Every day I wake up and never know whether I'm going to be treated like royalty or like a San Quentin prisoner. And every day I want to learn to play the piano. It would help if I had a piano. It's a complex, not-enough-instrumentals world. Sometimes I view it as a baseball game with swings more often than hits. But at least there's organ music officiating.

I've been a front runner for certain crimes and punishments. When my business partner and I had a wall design career, we had years of joyous jobs working in a field that was rewarding for us and for most of our customers. We got quite proficient in faux painting, doing everything from turning rooms into Tuscan villas to painting nurseries. Which included those re-do jobs when a client had to call back saying, "My baby can't sleep at night since you painted dinosaurs!" Another call back came regarding the faux bricks that didn't hold up to kitchen traffic. Or more specifically, the cast iron skillet that was launched during an argument.

We only had one client who exhibited some awfully blankety-blank behavior. Emphasis on awful. Her visiting mother described how her daughter is never happy. We were called to do specialty painting in their dining room, a technique with glazing that had to be applied a specific way. We had done this many times over, though she challenged our artistry. She finally agreed on our method then left us with her mother while she ran errands. Their radio supplied us with inspirational music, and we cheerfully worked while her mother watched over us with attentive satisfaction. Nearing completion, my teammate had to leave early to pick up her son so I told her I would wrap things up. The queen bee came home with nary a peep of appreciativeness. You would have thought we had finger painted swastikas all over her walls. The pestilent wrecking ball announced, "That's not what I wanted! You need to come back and redo this tomorrow!" I doubt her future dinner guests were going to gag on meals when their eyes wandered to our intricately painted artwork.

I wanted to be sympathetic, until the snarling resumed. Her mother revealed a thicker veneer of compassion when she whispered, "I love it." A payment check was handed to me by the disgruntled homeowner along with orders for our return. If this had been anyone else, we would have bent over backwards to make it right. But we didn't compromise with the irate. I sped out the door faster than a twin turbo jet and called my affiliate. "I'm on my way to the bank to cash this check. Will you call Mrs. Warmth & Wonderful and do your tactful dirty work of telling her we won't be back?" My associate, who was far more diplomatic than I was, knew how to dance around demands. Yet she replied, "That woman can go straight to the devil's paradise!" Had I known about it earlier, I would have recommended underwater screaming therapy that's so popular now with Angelina Jolie. Our client did have a pool. And together my partner and I had four hands. A dunk tank can be a good source of satisfaction. Since I wasn't fluent in foreign languages, I was fully prepared to converse in Pig Latin if she ever called again.

Post prima donna, we got a call from another client about her bathroom redo. We had become competent wall designers, yet not so competent at taking directions. The woman was not as callous a character as the last client, especially after the minor property impairment. It's not like we purposely went out of our way to torment anyone. But when my partner relayed the route to the destination, she told me to "look for the caution tape." Which was there, plain as day, alongside the house, and not blocking the entrance as previously designated. I pulled my car into the driveway and my colleague shrieked, "Back up! Back up now!!!" As I pulled away I noticed tire tracks imbedded deeply into wet cement. Boy was I in the hot seat. We sat there questioning why the tape wasn't barricading the entrance to the newly poured driveway. Never in my somewhat sizable cranial capacity did I think I'd be storing that scenario into my memory. Our sudden screeches brought the stunned, yet sweeter home owner outside. Needless to say we ended up doing that bathroom for free, plus offered up our firstborn children.

On a more playful occasion, the same partner in crime assisted me in an earlier restroom revamp. This time it was at a friend's home, and Ralph Lauren had just launched his trendy painting products. Our friend left for a few hours and came back to beautifully textured walls. We fancied ourselves as the faux finish queens on the cusp of a niche market. Except us interns still had some learnin' to do. I suspected all the other queens in the industry didn't have to call the company to ask questions. But there we were ready to dial the company since it was our first time attempting that particular wall treatment. My partner said, "I'll call the customer service hotline." There was a second extension in the same room so I picked it up to listen in. Our eyes bugged out of our heads at what we were hearing and we were doubled over laughing hysterically. We listened long enough to absorb the sensual experience. She had dialed one digit off and got the sex hotline by mistake. After feeling weak bladder bliss, we proceeded to do the job. I stopped her mid-fauxing and said, "We must tell our girlfriend what happened since she'll get the phone bill and think her husband or son made that illicit call!" These situations can manifest adversely, depending on the type of folks involved.

If we are to be inextricably linked to life's blunders, they would be much more manageable if they came with musical accompaniments, and a lot more mildly mannered people.

Orange Crush

I am grateful to say, that I have been happily adored in my life. My parents always loved me. I have friends who cherish me. Mosquito's absolutely adore me. And to many guys during my teenage years, I was the total package. They idolized me because they used to bring me their Christmas presents to wrap.

My first memory of being adored occurred when I was about six years old, by a devoted frog who lived beneath our bushes. Every day he would look at me with such excitation after I fed and caressed the little ribbiter. I kissed him, maybe with the ridiculous idea that he would turn into a handsome prince. My mother caught me in the loving act and assured me that he wouldn't be turning into a good-looking nobleman of royalty, and I would just end up with warts. Funny, but I've had one on the bottom of my foot ever since.

As a teen, life was good as long as no one asked me what my problem was, or about my love life. It was a little harder being adored when I had a bod that screamed beatitude, while those guys were much more interested in the high school harlots. Before I diagnosed myself with beggarly self-esteem, I first had to make sure I wasn't surrounded by twerps. One puerile adolescent tried coercing me into going to third base, and filling my belly button with Play-Doh. I didn't think I could stab any freakish dudes. Not when I could barely get my straw into my milk carton. But even bigger boy challenges were still ahead of me.

I did wish that studs would come along and keep it

simple, like kissing the hell out of me. When they didn't, I figured I could always scream to get their attention, get semi-nekkid at school assemblies, hire a professional matchmaker, or some combination thereof. God doesn't care how you worship. Although screaming is a very controversial action inasmuch as it has been known to cause certain complications such as people running from you, and frayed vocal chords. I worried about mine severing so severely that my doctor would keep them in a jar in his office to warn other patients of what can happen when you holler one-liners. Some words are just irretractable. I learned that it was better to just bat my young eyelashes.

On the flip side, I've had a few secret admirers. One boy in eighth grade had a crush on me but never had the guts to come right out and say so. I wondered exactly what it was about me that he liked, especially since I used a self tanner that turned me repulsively orange. Maybe he liked my hair. At the time, I had a long fluffy Ann Margret mane. Could have been the boobs. Mine also looked as corpulent as Ann's for quite some time until the gradual deflation. Who knew that bald sweater stretchers could pendulum so proudly. But back then, I was voluptuous. I probably could have given this guy at least two solid minutes of fondling fame. Yet I always wondered about the infatuation with fleshy protrusions that are ornamented with God-awful ugly udders. Our Maker could have at least decorated us with prettier spigots. And men could have other wild fetishes like gazing instead at camel humps. I'm sure camels wouldn't care as long as they were taken to dinner.

I kept imagining what this potential suitor liked to do since I wasn't into contorting in the back of an automobile, or putting a gross worm on the end of a hook. I basically wanted a clinger who could lavish me with regular rose delivery, and good morning plus goodnight phone calls, and have communication skills rather than simple stares. Besides one who could blow me kisses. Bonus points if he knew how to embroider and take trash cans to the curb.

 The crush became more apparent, though the shy Casanova needed nudging with a cattle prod. Then the day came when I finally received communication from him. My English teacher firmly believed that all correspondence should be checked and confirmed for proper spelling, content, tone, and also thought it was a superb idea to have another set of eyes proof documents for me. I know the boy was bashful because he sent me a message in a bottle, which my vial hungry instructor seized immediately. So I never knew what the folded paper said inside. I knew it came from this particular boy because every other guy in class was looking straight at me and he was looking up at the ceiling. The mocking songbirds chimed, "Patty and Tim sitting in the tree, k-i-s-s-i-n-g. First comes love, then comes..." yad-da yad-da yad-da. I felt those almost suicidal and homicidal tendencies running through my veins. They could have used less pain afflicting communication like Morse code, smoke signals, or cans connected by a string. Or better yet, silence. Not only was I unready for marriage or motherhood, I surely didn't endorse the deeds of my offenders. I too was a tongue-tied and clueless communicator who stared at the ceiling contemplating how I was going to get the bottle back instead of asking my admirer what he wrote. I also wanted to get my orange face back after it turned bright red.

 Eventually I did have a boyfriend who was very adoring and allowed me in the front seat of his car. He didn't care if my skin was orange or black or green. Yet the communication still wasn't perfect. We were at the mall one day when I signaled him from across the food court to get me a slushy drink. He brought me Chinese food. Since then, I've had some orange crushes of my own after seeing several handsome associates behind their aprons at Home Depot. My current love doesn't want me hanging out there anymore. He'd much rather have me crushing on orangey citrus when I'm making him juice.

Oldies but Goodies

I have quite the affinity for old people. I suppose I should start with my dad, the sprightly senior who at ninety-three, is still as sane as... well, not anyone I know over the age of sixty. But nobody would be after parenting a progeny of ten children. He was such a trooper. Especially the time he was so proud of me for killing my first spider in the bathtub. I live with the unfaltering belief that he was more besotted with me than bummed about the flaming shower curtain I lit on fire and reduced to ashes while burning the eight-legged perpetrator.

Resorting back to childhood can't be easy. Slipping into a vegetative state every day after lunch. Eating strained peas. Keeping candy hidden under the bed. The repercussions of no self control. The crying when the room is too cold. Or the many distractions that come with watching a motion picture. My most memorable experience with seniors came several years back when a buddy accompanied me to a home for the aged during their recreational movie night. Despite the commonality of benevolence, I wanted to show them *It's A Wonderful Life* when my compatriot suggested *Deuce Bigelow: Male Gigolo* or *Apocalypse Now*. I'm not so sure the seniors would have loved viewing memoirs of a pimped out person or experiencing perilous and increasingly hallucinatory journeys in their dreams that night. But it was the thought that counted. They favored my film over his unconventional mixture. Except that it was my own fault for showing a feature with a film length of two hours and fifty-four minutes and with an intermission time of forever, since we had to wait for the blessedly slow old man river to return to his seat after his potty break.

Into the second half, another gentleman decided to do a horizontal movie pause by drifting into a coma. If I didn't know better, I'd have to wonder if he mistook Vicodin for vitamins and swallowed them down with whiskey. And I love a man in uniform, unless that ensemble consists of boxers and a tank top with hair sprouting from every angle. I had to crawl out of the mire of discouragement at thoughts of my own impending destiny in senior housing with flashers and other peculiarities. I was however very much a supremely chic senior myself in golden browns, joining others in what looked like a turtle convention, since the spots on my carapace aren't so subtle as well. I was jealous of this individual's ability to snooze throughout the film and through one lady's full phone conversation with her daughter at a sound frequency only known to deaf people. God love her and her hairy male compadre.

Meanwhile, there was one more over-the-hiller waiting in patient preparation for me to pass around my bag of peanut M&M's of which I had every intention of hoarding. Surely he must have been aware that he had two candy bars of his own. But what do you do when a pensioning cutie pie looks at you with such an impassioned look on his face and a clobbering cane on his arm? I had to set aside that yearning inside my stomach to share. He told me of his fondness for both chocolates and hundred dollar bills. I would have handed over several banknotes with Benjamin Franklin if I had been much more closely connected to a treasury vault. I told him I would gladly help him out in my next life when I'm reincarnated as Bonnie Parker. I ended up giving the guy my yummy confections, and would likely keep this tradition of contributing if I could weed out currency extortionists and other chocolate lovers.

I remember one scene specifically, when it helps to associate certain situations with circus acts. Resident Ralph started flirting with Judith whose eye glass string got caught on Dorothy's wheelchair, which jerked spilling Judith's lemonade on Roy's pant leg which made him swear in Swahili just about the time Dolores sneezed on the attending caregiver, whose tray slipped sending a glass that Donald tried to catch but missed by eight feet, and the sugary liquid drenched the entire backside of Carl's toupee.

Benny had won at Cribbage hours earlier and was very verbal about taking his winnings and running off to Vegas with a gal he used to know, a person he talks about every day and who was apparently a very highly respected bar maid with implants. Mister sleepiness and candy snatcher decided to wake up and because he was directionless, needed help walking back to his room. I bid my crotchety relic of a movie date goodnight and then watched the fine fellow slide underneath his bed as if he was ready to repair an automobile. I wanted to ask if he had ever worked as a maintenance man at Goodyear, and if he did same day service. Come to find out, under the bed is where he hid his candy.

I fully 'fess up to my inner weirdness. So I am hoping my girls will see the humor in my aging process and patiently tend to my decrepitude when I leave my dentures in the refrigerator and my mind in the gutter. I'm rather hoping my own retirement includes a pension plan that will totally shape my emeritus experience. One that will cover an ocean soaring yacht with a crew that follows me around with a shaker of martinis and personal pan peanut M&M's.

My elderly friends aren't your stereotypical seniors. They are the most refreshing things since Glade was introduced to us. I called my eighty-three-year-old friend Ginny recently to go to dinner since we both like Mexican food, and because she adds such sparkle to my life. She informed me that she was too sick to go out. I asked what was ailing her and she replied, "I've got the rockin' pneumonia and my boogery grandson's flu."

This is why I love this lady. She is just as whimsically twisted as I am.

Rejection

Being rejected in fifth grade is typically normal. But some boys need to tactfully execute slicker Casanova techniques, so girls can be left quivering in their bodices, or crop tops, rather than feel lowly and defeated. Casanova's charm and irresistibility got him close to noblewomen, chambermaids, a nymphomaniac, and three unrepentant nuns, which truly says something about the scruples of certain vestal virgins. I doubt I'll be leading my granddaughter into a convent anytime in the future.

It was tormenting that no one invited my ten-year-old grand-darling to the grade school Masquerade Ball. I had a long discussion with the dissed debutante about the mating habits of halfhearted earthlings. Precisely, boys. She mustered up enough courage to ask a young stud herself. The boy hemmed and hawed at her request, and backed away saying he would think about it. Then with manners slightly undignified, he had another girl text her as a socially inept way of justifying why he couldn't take her and that he would be taking someone else. But he made sure she knew that she was second on his list. Clearly he had a vague misunderstanding of sensitive feelings. My granddaughter was pretty upset that she was snubbed, spurring the defense mechanism of simply keeping quiet. I was never a stalker, nor was her mother a stalker. I took total solace in knowing that she wouldn't be a stalker either. Although I do remember waiting for the lit can of hairspray to detonate under the chair of one slimy rejector. I'm kidding.

So much for kissing behind bleachers and honeymooning in Paris. It wasn't five minutes ago that my grandbaby thought boys stunk. Now she's in for the rough ride of consorting with the opposite sex. After hearing about her ordeal, and the fact that she went home and worked herself into a clamorous crazy-girl lather in front of her mother, it brought back memories of my own dateless despondency. I did have the violent impulse to take the incinerated remains of some boys and scatter them over a lion's den to make sure there was not a trace of them left behind. What parasitically infests the minds of refusers is beyond me. I want my granddaughter to have all the wisdom I never gave my own girls. Nurturing the voice of vulnerability, the first thing I told her was to get herself some armor to keep the hits from penetrating her heart. And secondly, not to run out and buy a sectional loveseat quite yet. The wedding venue will need a deposit first. Thirdly, I told her to soar with eagles rather than peck around with chickens. She was silent on the phone for a second, but I'm sure she mentally absorbed my meaning. Then I told her that I would always be around with a first aid kit if she decides to punch a chicken in the nose, or anyone else when faced with the potential of needing a bloody nostril.

It was time to apply *The Rules*, adapted from the popular book full of secrets on capturing the heart of Mr. Right.

Rule #1 tells you to be creative like no other. I would be inclined to say to any guy who dumped me, "Life is short, so I'll make this short. Finders Keepers." I believe Rule #2 states, "Don't talk to a man first or ask him to dance." It also stipulates how to act on dates 1, 2, 3, 4, through commitment. That is if she even gets a date to begin with. A girl could be going through menopause before she gets asked out. Rule #7 says not to accept a date for Saturday night after Wednesday. I'm not sure what takes guys so long. Especially ten-year-olds. Could be that they tire themselves shaving or looking for amphibians. Rule #16 points out that a girl shouldn't tell a boy what to do. She can't anyway. Not if there's a frequency of conversations when the male participant has ingested too much sugared lemonade. Rule #17 indicates that a girl should never take the lead. That's very true if he's going to the little boy's room. Although she could show him her infinite wisdom about personal hygiene by pronouncing that age old proverb, "If you sprinkle while you tinkle, be neat and wipe the seat." But I told her most guys already have mothers who tell them what to do. Rule #24 suggests slowly involving him with your family. So by the powers vested in me and my overprotectiveness, I now pronounce every potential villainous half-pint that comes within ten feet of my granddaughter or her loved ones, banned. Nixed. Possibly destabilized.

My granddaughter is angst ridden again knowing her mother is now her date. The boy should be equally angst ridden knowing my daughter is going to haunt him all night at the ball. I told her how combustible hairspray cans will be when there's a flame involved. I like to be as helpful as possible.

My daughter called me again inquiring, "Mom, you're crafty. Wanna make five masks for your granddaughter and four of her friends for the Masquerade Ball?" I asked, "When is it?" She said, "This Friday. So you have plenty of time to make them all tonight and get them in the mail by tomorrow morning."

Such pressure. I hope my daughter didn't feel too rejected when I told her she's out of her mind.

Worth the Wait

I feel pretty, oh so pretty. I feel pretty and witty and... surprised!

Let me start by saying that I have felt like something was missing in my life. I didn't know if it was a person, a puppy, or a cream puff. All those years I waited for Prince Charming to show up and thought the poor guy might be caught in traffic or something. When he didn't come, I ended up mating with the lively spirits of Schnapps and bourbon chocolate cupcakes, then bedded down with mister headachy nausea. I did learn that relationships are never a waste of time. If they didn't bring me what I want, it taught me what I didn't want. Although, I sure didn't want my body becoming a battered prisoner to an ever shrinking list of options. Destiny decides who we meet. But we decide who stays. I started the study of astrological compatibility and relied on the stars and planets to direct me. That strategy changed after reading that there has never been a Capricorn commingling of any importance and that I should just go kill myself. Instead, I resorted to adopting cuddly pets for partners. Dogs, cats, turtles, neighboring dogs, cats, squirrels. But similar to some of my dates, I found out quickly that they were much more interested in getting their hands on my food and they couldn't hold their licker.

After years of boyfriend shopping, I met my man. As you've gathered by now, I'm not one to reveal anything personal. It's enough that there are satellite pictures of my privacy, and I've been captured by cameras in stores everywhere. But I can't help sharing my jubilation. With the guidance of my girlfriend who was with me when I met him, and who had her doubts as well, he eventually got to both of us and proved to be surprisingly different. Not to mention he's fun, funny, has a generous heart, and wasn't pushy like your average bulldozer. Although the gun he keeps under his bed might be questionable. And it may be a contest which one of us is more entertaining.

This man didn't have me at hello. It took some doing and eventually a lot of push from my girlfriend. Early into this love tingle, this sister in shining armor stood straight up on my behalf. With her brows cocked like Clouseau, she threatened his life if he even considered cohabitating carnally too soon. A few dates into our relationship, I was suppose to stay at my girlfriend's condo after going to dinner with the canoodler. I called her to make sure she left me a key to get in. She overheard my verbally forward escort declare, "You can stay at my house." Knowing how the male psyche maneuvers, my protective pal overheard his proposal and screeched through the phone, "You let me talk to that man!" Because only a friend will love you like a sister, protect you like a mother, and kick him in the keister if he dared lay a hand on me. Mind you, other passive aggressive personalities would have simply asked, "What are your intentions?" I handed him the phone and she blatantly yelled, "Don't you dare touch her, buster!" She was always there to lead me through the dating forest filled with prospective predators. I felt a little like Red Riding Hood, and there might be another wolf standing in front of me, an entity to whom I would be nervously articulating, "My, what big ideas you have!" The last thing I needed was an animal. But he was simply a soul whose intentions were good and didn't want to be misunderstood.

Now one of two things could happen after his encounter with my prosecuting girlfriend. He would have the patience of a gentleman, or run for the hills. He was ballsy enough to hang in there. Except ballsy is just a euphemism for horny. I didn't want to stay the night for fear that either my snoring might ruin a potential relationship, or that intoxication might make some sort of magic happen. He had a philosophy that could potentially ruin any relationship. He kept his friends close and his beers closer. Too many brewskis made this man walk directly into a glass patio slider at the first family party, leaving his noseprint on the clear dense door. I certainly didn't need a significant other who was prone to drunken behavior. It's important to keep drinking under control because it can be the main cause of unpleasant glass or girlfriend attacks. I wondered if he had other deadly hobbies as well. Like cigarette smoking, or walking off curbs into oncoming traffic. Thankfully it wasn't just the Dos Equis lager: he couldn't see because he was in dire need of cataract surgery.

The guy did have one strange manly trait that made him stand out from the rest. He would rather be out with me than watch hockey. Now football is another story. But after awhile, it was my girlfriend who insisted, "Hang in there. He seems like a good guy." She was right, considering we had such fond memories of those first encounters. There was no need to jeopardize this union over a nasty nose welt, half blindness, or his hankering to watch a bunch of sweaty men on a field annihilating each other. With most dates, it was uphill in the beginning then downhill from there. With him, it was downhill at first, then he rose rather nicely to the top. And any man who talks tenderly about his mother was a keeper. The ultimate clincher to sealing the deal was right before the party when he chipped a tooth and super glued it against the other incisors so I wouldn't think he was an astonishing sight and severely lacking in a cohesive dental plan. He withheld being amorous but was hell bent on looking glamorous.

Before sex, I had momentary pity party about punishing the guy. So I had him show up at my house with me dressed in a trench coat. His heart went pitter-patter the moment I started to disrobe. I'm sure he hoped I would be wearing something skimpily laced, or wished I had been a lady of the evening in a former life. What he found was an extremely graphic expose of my arm and leg moles. I just wanted to show him the cute swimsuit cover I found on clearance at Macy's. Once my dear mister fantasy professed his love for not only me but the same tan lines, music, movies, and rustic breads, I sunk into a love so strong that a bond was being set. Sort of like epoxy with its reactive polymers. We also share the same commonality of major memory loss and foot cramps. We're a match made in pain hell.

This guy didn't give me that look that usually says, "Baby, I want you, but I also want every other female on the planet." But he had me wondering when he invited two other women to his house for fun Fourth of July festivities during our first summer together. Apparently they had nowhere else to go. Who was I to interfere with such boyish rituals? He sweated bullets at the thought of telling me before the party and said not to worry since one of them looked like Eyeore. I asked what the other one looked like, and he basically prayed that they wouldn't show up. His own son even asked what the heck he was doing asking women over. They didn't come. And I found out he really wasn't a womanizer. He was just being polite and likely wanted to show off his BBQing skills. That, or test me on how I would react to a ménage a trios with beauty and the beast. However harmless it was, I had to carefully monitor who his invitees were after that little bit of friendliness. A young buck makes his girl jealous around other women. But a gentleman makes other women jealous of his girl. My gentle man doesn't eye other gals, at least not when I'm looking. Nor did he ask if my sisters are hot. He's simply a very sweet social butterfly. Depending on the amount of sugar and alcohol he has in him, he is either selectively anti-social, or hardy-har-har funny and endlessly entertaining. I have never laughed with anyone like I do with him. Now I just need to hand him a list of my neuroses to see if he passes the test of true attachment. But as songstress Ingrid Michaelson describes, "He takes me... just the way I am."

P.S. My girlfriend adores this man and now wants a finder's fee.

Smartypants

An emphatic pounding startled me out of a deep sleep at 1:30 am. The next thing I knew, flashlight beams were scanning the sliding door, then penetrating my bedroom window. "It's the sheriff's department. Open the door!" I obeyed orders, the same way I obey the dentist when he asks me to open my mouth: very reluctantly. I unlocked my entry to three city officials who were operating their impressive instruments of communication. They saw the jolted look on my face, polarized by this sudden invasion of privacy. "We may have the wrong house. Are you Lucy?" My stunned state gave me the itch to respond in a smart-alecky and forthright manner like, "No! Are you Desi, Fred, and Ethel?" But I refrained. I was more prepared to say, "Okay already, I'll give back the butter knife that just happened to fall into my purse on the way out of the Italian restaurant last night." I suppose it was best that I didn't confess. But I probably looked like a criminal, because I sure felt like one.

What lampoonery when the police department can't deploy officers over the age of fifteen who can get their residences straight while making a house call. And because it was close to Halloween, how did I know these younguns weren't dressed in badged uniforms and holding onto fake firearms just waiting for me to pass out Mars bars in the middle of the night? It would have been different if my place had just become a crime scene, was filled with terrorist bomb making material, or if I was a Jello Wrestler gone wild and naked. The call was made because two people in the vicinity were squabbling. The worst part was the blinding flashlights and not being able to fall back asleep until after three am. When this sort of infiltration occurs, that's when sarcasm steps in. I wanted to suggest that a cosmetic clay derived from boar bristles can really cure their pimples. But I had another brand spankin new thought. Cops could make sure of the right address before waking the entire general area and quite possibly Nevada, besides making me look like a delinquent lawbreaker which could haunt me for the rest of my story-forsaken life. There was a lot more I wanted to say, but being tossed in the slammer would not have improved my perfect never-thrown-in-jail record. They could have arrested me solely on the look given during their final moments of interrogation. So far I have lived dangerously yet avoided that place behind cell bars where other smartypants provide gobs of sarcasm as well.

 I haven't been completely innocent. Call me the sneaky habitual harvester of natural plant life and manipulator of mail delivery. First of all, I have not known how to stop my ten fingered thievery since we are blessed with nature's finest wreath making deciduousness, along with irresistible cutlery that don a restaurant table. More recently I exited the library, and there stood a tree with awesome tendril relics dangling from it. I figured it would be a nice addition to my crime spree if I went back at dusk armed with snippers and a big bag. Why would anyone care? These droopy enticers probably grow back quicker than rabbits multiply. Butter knives I'm not so certain of. Sure as the smile on my face, someone showed up ready to wipe it away with the subtle insinuation that I might be doing something really, really horrible. I withheld the smugness of saying, "Unless you have handcuffs, I'm just gonna continue what I'm doing."

I'd like to become more of a criminal by slipping a bill back into the envelope and inconspicuously tape, staple, and glitter glue it back into its original form. Then write "No one lives here by that name" and throw it back into the mail slot, hoping it passes the postal inspection with all the fingerprints and foreign substances attached to it. I'd also like to pay my taxes in pirate treasure coins by shooting them via slingshot onto the White House lawn. I heard it's not hard to gain access anymore.

Here's another brain teaser. There's an X37-B mini shuttle that has been roaming around space and landed after a two-year classified mission. To do what? Spy on other countries? Or me? Let me get through a day without legislatorial interference. The next thing I know, they will be forcing me to wear polka dots on Wednesdays, and their secret snoopers will be scouring my rooftop for bird poop and up my waste management fee another 20%. Then they will be telling Charlie Sheen he can't date every cheerleader in Sherman Oaks plus half the waitresses in Los Angeles County. Though I might have to go along with the government when it comes to him. He's been so hooked on the hokey-pokey that I'm not so sure he can ever turn himself around.

Like Patsy Cline says, "Worry? Why do I let myself worry?" It's crazy to put the government in charge of, well, let me see... How about nothing! Need I remind probing constables of their own slovenly senatorial management? It's highly unlikely that I will get rid of my smartypantish attitude as long as someone is spying on me. They really have control issues. Take Massachusetts, where a district court judge slapped a five hundred dollar fine on a fisherman for untangling a whale from a net and setting it free. Apparently he didn't call state authorities first. They should be doing something far more useful, like solving our gravity problem. Newton's laws need to be repealed since my body is doing some awfully strange things. Plus, there isn't a lot of people living amongst us who are not that down to earth.

I used to fret that God might aim his lightning bolts and fry me at nine hundred miles per hour. But more realistically, the federal government may seize me and dump my lifeless body in a landfill. Which is already over-occupied with mattresses and men's golf clubs thrown there by disgruntled wives. These smarty Pattypants will more likely end up in purgatory. Hell is for people like Manson.

Patty Clark

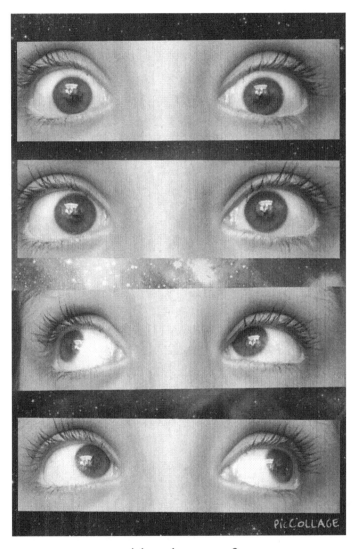

Granddaughter goofiness

Babelicious

I'm going to be a grandmother again. So are two of my girlfriends, and another one just became grandmammy of twins. That's what happens when young couples go messing around, or fly off to another country to undergo in vitro fertilization. At least an airplane ride and intrafallopian tube transfer can spare the neighbors the torture of hearing something else.

In the eighties, I always hoped I would get knocked up by watching *Magnum PI*. I wanted my children to be sired by Tom Selleck so they could have his strong stature and deep dimples. Plus I thought it would be nice to raise our offspring in the guest house of a posh two hundred acre beachfront estate and have Higgins to babysit. He seemed like the grandfatherly type. Well, that didn't happen. I raised my offspring in a cozy, quartered barrio shoebox surrounded by neighbors who never wanted to babysit. I suppose I haven't set a very good example for young women by saying I would have slept with Tom while I was married. But I'll betcha millions of his other women viewers would have put aside their guilt associated with the blessed sacrament of wedlock to do exactly the same thing. Perhaps I should be emphasizing the importance of a strong bond between two people. Not give a lesson on lust. But I gotta say, this child stuff starts with lust and continues with lust, when your every desire is be around that baby or grandbaby.

My first pregnancy, someone should have congratulated me on staying nine months sober. And while birthing, I was looking at a future already limited by pain and the failure to comprehend the arcane art of common childbearing, as if it was testing my endurance levels for teen exposure. I was a modest infant deliverer, and found it demoralizing retreating to a table disrobed. My doctor began breathing a bit heavier, so I assumed he either had respiratory problems, or a passion for expectant mothers. I shouldn't have worn perfume that day, or makeup.

Then the moaning began. I figured if Empresses of the 1800s were satisfied using chloroform while laboring children, I just knew it wasn't going to be good enough for me. I wanted something that would take the edge off for the rest of my child filled life. Or at least be inoculated with the highest quality palliative painkiller for slicing my privates and yanking out darling dumplings from my pressure cooker. But my epidural didn't take. The doctor said that when I stopped choking him, he'd do whatever he could to deliver the baby to me. He was somewhat gentle, a mild cross between my butcher and Edward Scissorhands. I grunted, groaned, cursed the ceiling tiles and the nurses who stood there acting like I was a complete wimp. I doubt these women were mothers.

A lady friend of mine said she never needed anesthetics. I asked her if she gave birth to ants. My mother told me, "This pain is the hardest to endure, and the easiest to forget." She had ten planned pregnancies, bless her poor strained body. It wouldn't have been so bad if my weebles hadn't weighed in at hippo poundage plus forty thousand ounces... kicking and screaming for some nourishment and a lifetime pass to Disneyland.

My sweaty experience was partly due to the dedication of... you probably thought I was going to say my husband. The daddio and meekly ministry of labor would have rather sat in a bar sipping brewskis than watch me scream. After a faint moment of falling over, I would have easily dabbed his lacerations with anesthetic. So I assumed he would be just as accommodating by sitting there nicely holding my hand. What I really wanted was Cheerios. All I remember is him saying, "It's three o'clock in the afternoon. Breakfast isn't for another eighteen hours." I would have fired him if he didn't have a family to support. It was time for him to go home and make room in his wallet for photos of another fine babe, relinquishing those pictures of Raquel Welch.

I took in all those live and learning fundamentals of parenting. My first daughter pooped mustard colored feces, and I frantically called the doctor. My second daughter pooped up a penny, and I started her future jean fund. My third daughter promoted literacy while pooping by reading Dr. Seuss over and over. The teen years were a tad harder. I knew not to have any more teenagers after the third one. Nora Ephron said it perfectly: "When you have teens, it's good to own a dog so someone in your house will be happy to see you."

Being a grandmother means living happily ever after. It's a time when we finally get parenting right and we can reap the benefits of adoration. I will never again be in grave danger of screwing up suppers or playtime activities. We provide good times, lots of treats, and know that only eggs can become rotten. The reason grandparents and grandchildren get along is because they have one common enemy in between.

My ten-year-old granddaughter announced that she'd like to visit me for a week, alone. When she comes, I need to remind her about human frailty. She already knows about Humpty Dumpty falling and that Jack tumbled down a hill cracking his head open. So she needs to be aware of something. If I'm going to jump rope with her or do some trampolining, she should remind me to wear a bra, and pad the cement.

Cold Turkey

It was my youngest daughter's first tackle at making Thanksgiving dinner. We had already exchanged holiday happiness earlier in the day. Yet when she phoned again mid afternoon, instinctively I knew that she still needed my motherly assistance. I hadn't noticed the call until two hours later. By the time I got back to her, the Epicurious had already called her older sister the more experienced Epicurean, who counseled her on doing things entirely differently than the way I had instructed. I could just see her frustrated face. She probably shouldn't take any advice from me next year either. Because I'll be suggesting that she save herself a lot of trouble and leave celebratory cranberry vodka shooters at the door with a sign that says: "Out to dinner, but drinks are on me." Except I wouldn't want to provoke a perpetual eye-roll from my offspring.

Uneasiness swept in when she told me that the two foil containers holding a ham and a turkey had holes in them and the drippings caused the fire. I was left with the vision of soot saturated table settings and all the potential meal attendees practically passing out from smoke inhalation and starvation. My daughter is a woman of confidence and great capabilities. She did manage to take the package of innards out of the turkey cavity first. And she stuffed and basted properly. When I asked her if she had eaten yet and she said it would be another four hours before they got to gobble, I could easily assume that she wasn't up slaving over the stove at five in the morning. I know how much she likes to sleep in. The suspended supper gave the fowl and the pig plenty of time to still claim refugee status. I didn't want to assume the possibility that she turned the oven on two hundred degrees, which would totally keep them from feasting until Black Friday. She could have speeded up the cooking process by upping the temperature to scorching degrees of flame inducing exorcism, leaving a sad state of un-scrubbable scorchness. Most of the dining delay came because she had to smother the flame and clean the oven. And, because her boyfriend with his infinite wisdom as a cookologist stood around telling her what to do. How he got both meats in the oven I'm not sure. I wasn't aware that he had an associate kiln-fitters degree. She said that she now understands why a cook doesn't need any extra bodies in the kitchen, and why she wore shorts and a t-shirt fanning herself while everyone else wore sweaters.

My daughter found herself enmeshed in the holiday tradition of making sure all the boys in her hood were filled with fowl. Truth be known, she only invited them for the amount of coins she knew would fall out of their pants and later be found in her couch cushions. After all was said and done, I can't imagine how my darling daughter ended up cutting the large bird knowing she has no sharp knives to speak of. She probably relied on someone carrying a retractable pocketknife. And I'm still wondering how the football team found parking in her driveway. I'm also surprised that while they were waiting to chow down, they weren't frying burgers and brats on the Hibachi in the backyard or ordering pizza. I would have been very worried about my guests going hungry and being fully vaccinated for salmonella poisoning. Not to mention a house full of smog dulling the senses. Maybe she wanted to see if the smoke alarms worked. Maybe she wasn't satisfied with the caliber of feral dinner guests that were arriving, or maybe she punctured the foil containers on purpose attempting to lure fire department hunks in uniforms to her house. But she was skillful in putting out the flames herself. I do believe this is how sepia photographs originated. Browned by the heat infiltration from oven infernos.

There's nothing like bringing out the best in family familiarity. When I was twenty-something, I remember the steps I took my first time cooking turkey dinner. I bought the bird. Then I had a glass of cheap wine. I stuffed the bird. Had another glass of cheap wine. Put turkey in the oven. Forgot to turn the oven on. Relaxed, drank, and socialized with visitors. Mistakenly went back to the bedroom to baste the turkey. Checked the internal temperature of the cat. Gave thanks for mom who was there and took over. To make matters worse, I think I asked my mother to stay longer and clean up. My reputation is still ruined after that dastardly day. But I figured the flurry of family was good reason for ingesting a reservoir of fermented beverages. Whoever says I can't cook obviously hasn't tasted my toaster strudel.

My daughter's beautiful baked bird showed up later in a picture text. The kid that never wanted to touch a kitchen tool as a teen has turned into quite the cuisine artist. I hope her day ended with an applause and a large amount of turkey leftovers. I love them. Turkey sandwiches. Turkey tetrazzini. Turkey soup. I draw the line with turkey à la mode. For Christmas, I am making sure she's equipped with heavy duty roasting pans, a carving knife, a fire extinguisher, a meat thermometer and muzzles. Then she won't be crippled in the kitchen, and will be fully armed against any cooking commandeers.

Nutcracker

I'm done with my Christmas shopping. Now before all you procrastinating people curse the fine paper you're reading from, hear me out. A year ago I was hemming and hawing at the indignant early appearance of Christmas decorations in stores that have the luring potential of getting us to prepare far in advance for gift giving. I delayed the exercise of intensive mall duty until my eagerness reached a much higher level. But I figured the following February would be too late. I drove to the marketplace of indefinite dimension where I saw Santa and his merry men obstructing traffic to and from Nordstrom's. Or at least that's what I told my daughter who wanted a gazillion dollar Dooney & Bourke purse. I'm sure she ended up squealing with delight after seeing gift certificates for Panda Express under the tree. After a rancorous evaluation of my finances, I began feeling nothing but contempt for mall chislers who charge exorbitant amounts of currency for their goods. Though instead of shopping for others, I realized I should be shopping for myself. My mother's words tend to resonate... "Always have on decent underwear, shoes, and jewelry in case you get into an accident." So off I went to Macy's.

There were plenty of cologne sales people taking up every inch of aisle space as I headed towards the shoe section. One clerk tried to transmit glad tidings through her hoarseness, which was released with bronchial bacilli and followed by a force of phlegm. She sprayed enough cologne on my wrists to exude suggestive nights on a street corner. After going through the germy perfumed preliminaries, I was pretty sure I would contract something bacterial, and was hoping that she wouldn't want to play Patty-cake or hand wrestle with me. I'm not sure why salespeople who are coughing up sales pitches while thrusting viruses on you are still employed. But I wasn't buying. Or staying. She didn't succeed in making me purchase something that will sit on a shelf with fourteen other unexplained substances that have been stored there since the seventies. This is when I want department stores furnishing face masks. And it sure wouldn't hurt if Jamba Juice and Wetzel's Pretzels had a liquor license.

Parking is like bracing yourself for another wintery wallop. I was compelled to nag stores into saving me a spot and validating for the last two months of the year. I realize that moving to California would provide cultural differences. But I never thought I would need to carry around nerve gas when dealing with drivers. It's okay to steal someone's spot if you don't mind retaliatory crowbar dents on the hood of your car.

It tickled me pink to wait in line at Toy's-R-Us on Thanksgiving eve while drinking my dinner, a smoothie blended with turkey, mashed potatoes, and cranberry sauce. I had just given thanks for everything when a dudish dragon with a girl tattoo slid in front of me who was more than willing to start a stampede and race for the same doll that I wanted. I had never seen someone so spirited. I have honed my people skills, but it's my intolerance for line cutters that needs attention. Sometimes you just need a sledgehammer to crack a nut. I love the male species, but when it gets to the point that their primal instinct is to battle for something and race to the front of a line, it makes me want to achieve a heavyweight title. As a good character assessor, I thought he'd be much better off embalmed. Thinking more rationally, I should have stood in line with a pallet of Snickerdoodles and a thoroughly rehearsed story of why I needed the doll more than he did. As it was, I was waiting there so innocently reading a Thessalonian's *Guide to Patience* book. Not really. It was a decoy covering. What I was truthfully reading was *Act Like a Lady, Think Like a Man*.

Once the store opened, I was hoping the pusher would stop and ask me for aisle directions. I would have led him straight out the back door. The guy got the doll first, and probably shattered the dreams of about two hundred other poor souls including me. It was his word against mine. But I was taught to excuse and endure whatever comes. After the initial paralysis wore off, I was never again going to stand in a line that long and end up manic depressive over something that was sold out. I might have three minutes when my affection for gifting swells. But all of this prompted me to move away from the common practice of cramming to Christmas shop plus pushing through a treetopia of mad dashers and vixens. Those not-so-brief moments of crystal clarity led me to buy Christmas presents all year and be finished shopping by the end of the autumn season.

Women were born to shop. This girl now abides by that persuasion between the hours of January 1st through October 31st. Besides, it's not economical spending in November and December. That coat I bought myself last year cost a bundle. I have tried keeping up with both the Pottery Barn and Crate & Barrel standards of living. But their goods could cost me roughly five thousand dollars when I only have fifty. This year, my lunch bag luminaries will provide ample direction to my doorstep. And people partying at my place will be using the finest in decorated plasticware. I hope my leftover Fourth of July napkins will suffice. I think the stars on them still work, and I have made George Washington look more like a jolly bearded St. Nick. I would have liked hiring the Detroit Symphony Orchestra for entertainment, but the Chipmunks will do. They ran out of mistletoe, so I'm hanging mustard greens. Though my strings of lights might not be untangled until Easter. All my pre-bought presents are ready for wrapping, and I've developed OGD (Obsessive Gifting Disorder) since I bought more than I remembered I had. Budget cutting cannot apply when there are Christmas sales in July.

Temple of Doom

♥

"Mirror, mirror, made of glass... tell me I've got the greatest cheekbones ever."

The mirror is a reflective phenomenon to which I allocate very little value. It used to be good for making funny faces. Now mine says, "WARNING! Object in mirror may appear older!" They are meddlesome mechanisms designed to contort us into something we aren't. And never will be. At least that's a conversation I continue to have with myself. The rest of me is in an agonizing crisis situation. Cyrano de Bergerac was a gifted strong-willed individual who was the prime subject of ridicule with his large nose, yet still fought for love. I have a fairly large gray area in my head, so I'm similarly fighting for something as well. Like lucidness.

I'm not here to talk about my body, or de Bergerac's. Just my mind. Which is resting atop of this fine monolith of feckless flab. People are already calling my girlfriend sidetracked Sally since she gets distracted. Next they'll be calling me preoccupied Patty. Middle-agers do everything we can do to stay sane and focused, while convincing ourselves that we aren't deteriorating into doomsville. It's a question of mind over matter, and who is the best lipo-surgeon in town. It cannot guarantee to prolong our lives but can guarantee our thighs will look darn good in a graveyard. If someone could just devise a plan to keep brain cells from going bonkers and ice cream from cultivating cellulite.

Mental mystifications began back in grade school. How does the landing of Christopher Columbus have anything to do with maturing? Or parenting? Because what I learned should have been more helpful once I was grown and was trying to combat imperfections, and my first born was spinning paper clips in the microwave. School put this awful pressure on us to figure the square root of fourteen, when I really needed to know how many liters of soda I should have for a party of thirty-eight, or fifty, if friends bring friends. Furthermore, they should teach children in classrooms how to serve mommies breakfast in bed without messing up the whole dang kitchen and getting grape jelly all over the sheets. It shouldn't take me a millennium to comprehend mathematically how to do a diamond wall pattern. But it took nearly that long when my wall design business partner and I went to outline a client's bathroom that wasn't perfectly square. My focus wasn't always on ratios and variables. Educators should have taught us all about that, along with skirting boards and cornicing. Luckily three heads are better than one. Mine, my partner's, and the homeowner's. The resident held the manometer while we the professionals measured. This instrument was much needed, since it detected the pressure of gas in the atmosphere.

That job took eleven days, nine hours, and thirty-two minutes to complete. It would have been quicker if the homeowner had previously scrubbed down the walls, and we didn't have to stop to call our kids, consult the mirror for wrinkles or paint in our hair, snack, or watch Oprah. My affiliate and I had a contest on who would eventually acquire the most facial creases. I haven't seen her in quite some time. But I'll guess I've outnumbered her by fifty. Thousand. I'd have less if my teenagers hadn't fought over things. I take that back. She probably has more. She had six kids, and I only had three.

I look at the longevity of my father. At ninety-three, he is golfing, going to the gym, and is still able to steady a martini. Most other people his age are lounging passively in recliners and holding onto bathtub safety bars trying to hoist themselves up. You can find my father gleefully perspiring through challenging greens, milking every possible putting minute as he sinks balls into the ground and likely swearing under his breath if his stroke is slightly off. This is otherwise known as purposeful living. You know, making those tough choices between ordering a simple after the game Tanqueray and tonic, or a drink a bit more detailed. On the rocks with Italian vermouth, lemon juice, dash of bitters, 1 c. ice, then shaken and strained to perfection. Elders can be such troublemakers.

Where was I going with this?

Perhaps we can finally concede that Cyrano de Bergerac didn't let a mirror and his proboscis head obstruction get in the way of pursuing his passion. Except that his passion was put on hold to go spend countless hours searching for items in grocery stores. Columbus made it to the free land. But he lived on fruits and veggies and wasn't concerned with rapid aging or finding the Hamburger Helper. I do have the brainspan to remember my birthday, meal times, and where I live. But there was the time I went cross-countrying by car and veered towards downtown Duluth, then found myself in El Paso. I've spent a third of my existence counting age spots and standing in places wondering if I was meant to be there. It does make me curious when I've lived in a perpetual phase of transportation. With a little luck, I will age like my dad and not be a troublemaker. Although the golfing gene is not hereditary. I need a putting hole the size of Shea stadium, and the only wedge

I know is a salad. But hopefully I will still know what Tanqueray is at ninety-three, and hope I don't give off caustic and unmistakable scents of Ben Gay and pureed cauliflower. I have already started using a pill caddy that I use for sorting earrings and Skittles. And know that soon I will be one of those drivers who will likely get passed up by a snail. Cyrano only lived to be thirty-six. But nothing could beat his wit and panache. So there should never be the pressure for me to attend Princeton. Not when my temporal lobes are filled with aphorism and so many street smarts.

Oz-Servations

My boyfriend and I were in the car one day making all sorts of observations. We couldn't for the life of us figure out why the road commission decided to refresh the dividing lines with paint during rush hour traffic. I began chiming, "If I were queen of the forest, I would basically command each worker to do their duties during our sleep time." My beau replied, "But how do you talk to authority figures who don't have brains?" I said, "It's simple. I would takeover whatever Wiz that was, whereupon I'd woof and woof with a royal growl woof, then click my heels and have them do what I say, or else I would order a flying monkey attack."

Not every pusillanimous creature that crawls the earth has a cerebral cortex made of straw. Mine is composed of mush, probably due to all the malignity I see on the highways. Like motorcyclists who come up silently from behind and scare the lunch burrito out of me. Then there are those whose backfiring exhausts sound like gun shots. Lions and tigers and bears peruse these pathways as well flashing their middle fingers to other drivers, which might be the international hand sign for "you idiot." You don't know how many times I've wanted to gesture back my own fist action and shout, "Put 'em up, put 'em up!" I'm sure these folks are practicing followers of Germanic neopaganism. On this particular day, we were practicing followers of gawkism. We passed one unpopular roadside attraction where two people in their parked pick-up were totally exerting themselves by sitting in a kama sutra position. Now that takes guts. Or third degree lust! Such an odd place to produce offspring. They probably read a sign half a mile behind them that said, "Hump Ahead." Since we had slowed down for the precarious event, another aging driver passed us screaming, "Use Ya Dam Blinka!" I think my boyfriend wanted to kiss old yeller with the grill of his Audi.

Speaking of rebel rousing, my man proceeded to drive me through his old stomping grounds, showing me where he skipped school and loitered around the streets. I got a very vivid idea of his former life when he mentioned more of the pranks he and his friends pulled. He was far more likely to have an accident when he was taking down mailboxes with his moving vehicle. He did save a lot of money on his car insurance though, by switching to eighty miles per hour and leaving the scene. I'm not so sure he is going to make it somewhere way over the rainbow when he croaks because because because because because, because of the wonderful things he does. After witnessing some of his fiendish shenanigans myself, I'm surprised he doesn't have a witch soaring high above him writing "Surrender" in the sky.

I don't remember Dorothy running across litter on her journey to Oz. What makes a muskrat guard his musk? Courage. And what makes drivers dump trash from dawn through dusk? Audacity. We weren't in Kansas. We were in a highly traveled metropolis full of constant littermeisters. Not transporting ourselves in an untainted surreal landscape of yellow brick roads en route to an Emerald City! I felt like a scarecrow sauntering through slums with barred windows, where I'm sure The Lord's Prayer is spoken frequently. My beau said jokingly, "Don't let the barbed wire and graffiti fool you. This is a nice area." After driving around awhile, I realized there was more of an urgency to skedaddle. I wished my boyfriend's car had a piddle-ometer that would point us to the nearest public restroom since peeing is prohibited on street corners. If happy canines can urinate on fire hydrants, why oh why can't I? The way I see it, there are two types of women in the world. Those who hold it, and those squatters who bare their buttocks to open fields and risk getting bit by bugs or wiping with leaves of poison sumac. It was then that I decided to start carrying around those added necessities in my purse. An empty coffee can, a roll of toilet paper, and a small tent for privacy.

Continuing on into a construction zone, road crews really should alert us about one mile beforehand of their re-routing advisories. They could schedule it on a simple billboard in very large fluorescent print surrounded with massive blinking lights, because we almost ended up in Mexico. It prompted a rich discussion between us, and I told him, "Pay no attention to those men behind the border." I figured if they liked us, they would let us return to the US. If they didn't like us, we would be under arrest and have to stay in a cellblock for God knows how long. Since my mate thinks I am a species not necessarily native to our own environment, he calls me his legal alien. We had the brains to figure out that there are penalties for illegal immigration. We saw border officers prudently patrolling with guns, and I was almost positive I heard them chanting, "Oh-we-oh... you ho." An image of the cowardly lion kept popping up into my mind. My boyfriend, the wonderful Tinman, turned our chunk of metal around, and got us out of there. I must say that it was a good entertainment replacement for Netflix.

Sometimes I think I should be a part of the department of transportation planting poppies along the highways to get speed demons to slow down. One wicked witch of the west sped right in front of us, who was very likely driving a stick. Attached to a broom. There was no car space to merge into, yet the stretch behind us could easily fit two Apollo moon modules, a five hundred passenger train, plus a blue whale. What's the hurry? Sometimes the first step to forgiveness is understanding that the other person is a frequent flying disaster waiting to happen. My talented and dedicated driver used some rather creative cursing then decided to curb his car. He is always claiming, "There's no place like home."

Calls of Duty

One of my first jobs was driving one of those mobile hot dog trucks in Florida after I graduated from high school. Hundreds depended on me to fulfill their frankfurter dreams, which basically meant standing around yawning while waiting for someone to show up. I had unlimited access to fast food for eight excruciating hours. It's a wonder I eat hot dogs today. My resume looked spectacular, despite the fact that they had to eliminate about fourteen pages of what I blew out of proportion. But I had tons of experience after serving my nine siblings pigs-in-blankets for a vast number of subservient years throughout my teen existence. Truth be known, I believe I got the job based on my bustiness at the time, which has now deflated substantially. It wasn't long before I had to rely on whatever brainpower I had.

During my lengthy two week stint driving the weinermobile, I parked the vendored vehicle on a car dealership lot and never knew who I was going to serve that day. The hungry drive-bys, the ecstatic new car owners, or the disgruntled car salesmen who needed to close deals. One day I encountered the disgruntled drive-by. I was loading on his double mustard when he asked me, "Don't you know who I am?" I looked him up, down, and sideways before answering, "Not a clue." Moments later, I didn't think a hot dog would evoke such resentful emotion. I wanted to ask if he had a few hours to spare while pondering his identity. Working with the general public sometimes squeezes the good nature right out of a person. I had rather deep insight to his kind of human suffering and did two things. First of all, I kept a Pez dispenser on hand to boost the gaiety of crestfallen customers. Secondly, I joined a support group to comingle with other pity partiers who loathed their occupations. We met twice weekly at a bar.

I should have told the all-star to take my lack of football player knowledge to the complaint department. But Mr. Football Famousness left briskly without even so much as thanking me with a tip. I disliked that job for several reasons. Waking up. Certain customers. Wearing a bra for eight hours. Having mustard stained shirts. Measly pay. And the pressure of exactly how much relish should cover a cylindered piece of meat. Pretending to be pleasant all day got pretty exhausting as well. So I moved on to bigger and better things. My true calling was hanging out with my friends and shopping. Except that I needed money to do that.

Career plans were way more exciting when I was four. At seventeen, I thought about being a flash dancer. But I was afraid mom and dad wouldn't take too kindly to me sauntering on a stage naked and whipping myself around a pole in front of strangers. I knew I wouldn't want to glaze pigs at Honeybaked Hams and leave their premises reeking of brown sugar and corn syrup. And woe would be me if I worked at a movie theatre tearing tickets. I wouldn't be able to contain myself when revealing all the movie endings. After graduation, I surely didn't want to work for any corporation that has their own unique way of doing things, which was usually their way. After all, I have an opinion or three. I wasn't cut out to be a cubicle girl. Those places require the work of three women and I could totally foresee an army of problems marching before me. In which case I would have had to fill the lunchroom sinks with pots of espresso and antidepressants, dunk my head in, and drink excessively until it was bone dry. I couldn't get that at any Starbucks. No additives in coffee, no desire to workee. Besides, they could fire me citing unaccountabilities. Although other careers would be far more hazardous to my health, like a rattlesnake handler or a high-rise window washer.

The parents said I could be anything. I ended up an artsy, madcapped, maternal patrol officer with major phobias. Which was mostly a fear of kids and their opinions, secondary to pointed objects and manic scares of manipulation. There was a time when I thought about being a flight attendant. Instead, I stayed grounded with children. But thoughts of sky soaring never left my mind. While feeding my babies in their high chairs, I taught them to make sure their tray tables were in the upright and secured position. I did find out that mothering was no different from being a cabin attendant since I catered to restless attitudinal mortals who were always pushing my buttons. I encountered turbulence and wondered if I would ever make my connection. My mother even told me, "Tighten your brastraps. It's going to be a very bumpy ride." There was one difference between the two careers. An attendant can do all that she does for eighteen hours and still look good. I looked like a wartorn Raggedy Ann.

In order to improve my productivity, I did regular Richard Simmons workouts. I basically rubbed up against the television tube hoping his energy was contagious. I didn't know whether to model myself after Donna Reed, or use some of Roseanne's rationale. I did maintain a job while mothering. And in doing both, I ended up failing at many things. Tried to get both myself and the kids ready and out the door in ten minutes. Failed. Tried to keep a daily diary of their growth patterns. Failed miserably. Tried to contact Duncan Hines to tell them yellow is not a cake flavor. Failed to get a response. Tried getting my kids to listen to me. Response failure mounting into the thousands. I must have totally forgotten to teach my sweet youngest child o' mine how to sew after noticing her stapled pant bottoms when her hems came undone. But look at the highly achieved Hugh Hefner. In 2005, he tried and failed to create a no nudity version of Playboy featuring a Miss World contestant on the first cover. It's just impossible to live without failing at something.

My life has been one long series of waking tired and going to sleep wide awake. I have a job, but don't have kids keeping me up at night. Yet I awaken anyway because childbirth destroyed my bladder. Based on my calculations, I can pretty much retire ten years after I die. I have spent two thirds of my life looking for a career that would make me happy, and make me millions. Because I know I'd be pretty darn good at it.

Exfoliation—so essential!

My Four Hours of Fame

Stardom is a many splendored thing for those of you who thought it might be love. Love is only included if you're making ten million dollars per film and you've got a barge sized, air conditioned trailer for resting in between shoots.

In an all too brief period in my past, I got a call to be an extra in a Verizon commercial. I'd like to point out that it was my four infamous hours of derogation, which gave me unrealistic expectations about ever getting a CAA award for commercial acting. It was probably the one hundred and fifty buck payment that I wanted at the time, and a teensy wonderment of the starry life. They could have gotten a known Hollywood actress to do it, but it would have likely cost them one hundred and fifty thousand. Instead, they called me. I'm sure it wasn't my looks or my not-so-formal training in theatre arts that got me the coveted role. So many of us have the word "sucker" written on our profiles. I did wonder if this was how Elizabeth Taylor got started. Although I was pretty certain it wasn't how porn stars began their illustrious careers.

I arrived at the designated site and was re-directed to a desert ranch, then rerouted again by bus to the actual filming area in the middle of flipping nowhere. What I didn't know was that I was one of approximately two hundred extras, which basically made me a microbiotic speck in the crowd. We were divided up and standing patiently atop two arid alps, sweating profusely, waiting for the megaphone's yell of "Action." Talk about being hot in suburban Hollywood. It must have been a hundred-degree day and my Lady Speed Stick decided not to provide me with proper perspiration abolishment. I guess I was going for the simmering sautéed look, standing next to others whose shower power and deodorants weren't working as well. But this wasn't exactly the time for product comparison.

They wanted a diverse group, so they gave us several choices of things to wear. Tuxedo, evening gown, casual wear. It was a good thing I picked casual wear and not a tuxedo. Black and intense heat result in clothing-to-skin fusion. But I swore Satan was there and brought his weather with him. I should have crammed my upper mounds into that much needed sports bra. However they did say to wear close toed shoes. That's because sticks and stones could break my lovely toe bones and desert rats could use them for snacking. Several girls decided to go with the glam look inside their full-length formal dresses and heels. I took every opportunity to thank the dear Lord for steering me towards a sleeveless top and sneakers. With all the heat suffocating togetherness, one guy keeled over from dehydration while another turned swiftly, trying to catch him, and almost knocked out my front tooth. Teeth are very important if I want to look ravishing on red carpets or eat meat, and if I don't want to appear homeless.

All of us were ordered to charge down these huge hills towards one particular person who was holding a cell phone. It would have helped if that person had been Jimmy Smits, giving me a larger bit of motivation. At one point of good audio confidence, the main character yelled, "I can sure hear you now!" How could he not hear the storm of ignominious, two-legged creatures aimed right for him. I finally understood the term "cattle call" when we looked like a large herd of livestock dizzily stampeding and stirring up dust, along with avoiding tumbleweeds and wild critters and producing an extraordinary public display of respiratory wheezing. It was good training for when I become a trespassing rancher, or a cow chewing my cud and qualifying as the laughing stock. I'm sure I spoke for a lot of us when I yelled back, "Can you talk into my good ear? The left one is loaded with soot!" I was told earlier that day to respect my fellow smelly stampeders. But a cattle prod would have come in strappingly handy. I wanted to be insured by the mafia since their slogan is... "You hit her, we hit you."

My repeated cries to get recliners for in between takes went completely ignored. I wasn't the only one who showed up with a workplace gripe. One guy wanted pizza delivered and overhead sprinkling systems installed. Speaking of nourishment, vendors were set up selling foods that were death threats. I simply wanted to be sipping something very wet and succulent. I was pretty sure it was martini-thirty somewhere. We were lucky if we got water.

We must have galloped up and down those hills ten times. Trying to stay focused on the onerous task at foot, it seemed clear enough that I was hanging on to this simmering spotlight by a breakable thread. By the time we were finished, we all looked like red-eyed emaciated migrant workers from Death Valley. I received the lovely parting present of a sinus infection that took the bulk of my paycheck after visiting my doctor. The day did nothing to initiate feelings of wealth or stardom. Although it did initiate the need for getting off my sore feet and soaking in hot sudsy bath water. I held out hope that I would see just one strand of my windblown hair in that commercial. As it turned out, I only saw the commercial once and never saw myself in it. I take that back. I was the one running. We did totally resemble a cattle drive, only the trail boss wasn't riding a horse. He preferred leading the pack from his luxury limo.

Even if I were to get another job offer that requires running and sweating on the set, I'd have to tell them that from now on I will get my four hours of fame the normal way. Under surveillance cameras at Target.

Man Caving

I spend a lot of time at my boyfriend's house. Before I collected enough bravery to forge forward into the mighty man cave, there were things worth investigating. Like if he showered. Or if he kept a clean house. And his bedding. Cotton? Satin? Former girlfriend? I knew I wouldn't find any potpourri. And did he grill? I have this persistent condition that keeps me from starvation. It's called hunger.

If I had wanted to lose this guy in ten days, I would have used the reprehensible tactics of showing up at his place with flowery needlepoint pillows and wedding magazines while whining incessantly. Or, I could have simply placed a scorpion inside his bedsheets. But because he was a keeper, I chose to hold off on the whining and revealing my mean streak. This man is definitely life imitating art, thus living in beautiful surroundings and setting off a series of elaborate delectables from the outside rotisserie. Every brushstroke of barbeque sauce is his art form, and I am in awe of his established patterns of preparation. Before I delve any further into his awesomeness, I still had some concerns.

Opening anything inebriating and drinking it can alter his main meal responsibilities. In a split five minute distraction, ye old grillskeeper can char meat if he has inhaled his fair share of spirits and wanders away. It wasn't too difficult deliberating whether or not I wanted my future dinners to be medium rare or seared to the point of calling the fire department. So I reminded the roaster that the grill clock is ticking. I wouldn't want to read visitants their last rites. Local funeral homes are holding my pre-sworn affidavits in case of botulism or fatal well-doneness. But my man has potential. First of all he has only incinerated the meat once, and I've had some pretty spoiled brats. He does keep the phone number for a good pizza parlor available. Yet he will never have the light-starved stagnation of a cold grill. I did want to send him to a college that offers degrees in eco-friendism and folklore studies, so he doesn't repeat the same old stories. Hopefully our garden parties won't take a dreadful descent when my man brags about being politically conservative.

The man cave doors are always open to the patio, so it's nothing to walk into a room and see a curious coon staring up at me. I'm sure they are drawn in by the waft of charcoal broiled scents. Their visits are such happy ones that I jump up and down with agitation. Then I shoo them out just as I do birds and cockroaches. My sweetheart told me he needed to call the exterminator, for the fiftieth time. Looking for the number, I risked disease opening his drawers to crud and rodent droppings. I would hate to be hospitalized for hantavirus. I'm just grateful the man washes his dishes and wears clean clothes.

Rest assured though, the resident ambassador of indoor plumbing has fresh towels to accommodate bathroom attendees. But lawn weeds have popped up all over the place like pimples on adolescents. The bastion of manliness sounded like a broken record when he declared, "I've got to call those lawn people." Knowing his humor, he'll probably ask me to pull a few of the buggers in exchange for drinks, grilled meals, sleeping accommodations, and swigging his wine.

Those man cave drinking rituals began rubbing off

on me. You can lead a horse to water, but she might prefer several smooth Cabernets. While pouring he tells me, "Say when." I can't ever seem to say, "Stop." Thankfully the kitchen didn't flood. Although there have been times I've been on the floor sopping up fermented remains as well as trying to get some back into my glass. Waste not, want not. It's never a good idea to get bombed during side dish gestation. Interestingly enough, walls tend to start moving by themselves. I never feel particularly inspired scouring my boyfriend's kitchen floor, which is basically the craziest thing I've done in the name of love and inebriation. I find myself delivering slurred soliloquies on how not to screw things up during dinner development. He likes kisses in the interim. Except embracing can lead to varying degrees of difficulty, like the sight of a hickey. In which case, I'd have to cover it with a turtle neck in eighty-five degree weather to avoid embarrassing comments.

Another downside to man caving is that you can gain twenty pounds sitting in a lawn chair gobbling on grilled goodies and leave needing liposuction. My belly suddenly drops like a feed sack. I end up having my beau wrap a large beach towel around my waist and shimmy it at the speed of however fast he can turbo twist the fat away. He doesn't worry like I do. He occupies his time thinking up his next grub grilling concoctions. The kind of higher superior who created grilling cannot be the same maker who came up with sagging skin. When I praise my guy on his six-pack, he knows I'm referring to his brand of beer.

Now that the king of the cave has made me a queen-like integral invitee, I have given it some rather codified girlie touches. I do think we make a tightly knit twosome. And on most days, his place seems to be engulfed with nothing more than his sweet beau-ish company, the strums of his guitar, and looking at the grill wondering who is going to clean it. Before ruining my sterling status as his girlfriend, he should know that I don't have the controlling desire to take over his barbequing enjoyment. Nor do I own a scorpion.

Sh Sh Sh Sh Sh Sh Sugartown

On one hand, I feel a tremendous sense of sympathy for my eldest daughter, caused by the fact that she held a slumber party for my granddaughter in celebration of her tenth birthday. Which in recollection of my past party experiences, was probably the only time I wanted to chug Drano. If I had to do it today, I would be filling a prescription for Xanax and popping them like Reese's Pieces.

On the other hand, what goes around comes around. My daughter claims she never had a sleepover. I beg to differ. I vaguely remember several pre-teen rabble-rousers stomping through my petunias and powdering their noses with my baking soda. Beyond that is a blur. Except that my neighbor Delia came over to calm my nerves by throwing me a life preserver, and wanted to fill the piñata with worms. Plus have a scavenger hunt, sending the kids off to the next county. She didn't have children. Go figure.

If my memory serves me, one particular partygoer who preferred not touching water altogether and had essentially the same motor skills as a tortoise, squandered precious festivity time away by picking her scabs rather than play sprinkler musical chairs. And here I thought it was so ingenious of me to provide such fun game playing. I wanted all the sleepless girls to play the lie-still-and-watch-a-movie game, which was ideally suited for a hyped up cupcake crowd. Some of the girls wanted to see a scary film. The others bucked that idea knowing their parents weren't around to clutch onto. That's when the bickering began. But some pre-teens are less likely to be governed by an overnight hostess such as myself.

I once believed that I lived in the wonderful world of cute dresses, butterfly kisses, and the idea that girls matured faster than boys. That was until the sleepover. Eight girls together aren't always sugar and spice. It's more like boogers and lice. I still had two younger girls who would soon be eager to have the same soiree. Now I understand my mother's perpetual disdain for erratic behavior in adolescents, limiting our parties to three hours despite the biological compulsion to trade us all in for pets. As a teen, she told me that I wiggled when I walked and that I should wear a girdle. If only she could see these young girls today baring thong straps and bosomy tank tops.

I'm sure my daughter wanted to undergo elective surgery and have her ears sewn shut for that twenty-four-hour period when she hosted her child's slumber party. From what I understand, she filled goodie bags in preparation for the event, when my granddaughter demanded one for herself with a sort of gimme disquietude. She wielded serious powers of persuasion towards something as insignificant as party favor sacks filled with dollar store items. Suffering the pubescent outcry, my rather rational daughter told her, "You're getting seven much larger presents. Isn't that way better?" Supposedly the pouty one still wasn't satisfied. She could be walking through the marvelous maze of Disneyland with Mickey giving her his undivided attention yet her focus would still be on birthday party goodie bags. The experienced parent such as thyself can surely empathize. Although it could have been worse. My granddarling could have said, "Gimme a bag now or else!" But she didn't. That's because my granddaughter is perfect in every way.

The integral part of the party began with present opening. Her mother was glad she didn't get an Easy-Bake-burn-yourself oven or a Razor scooter with no helmet. The youngun' wanted a palomino, because every delusional child wants a horse and stable and several acres to ride the neighing animal on. When one wasn't outside wrapped and waiting for her, unwrapping soon became a substantial waste of her opening enjoyment.

Thus began the pilgrimage to the tent of terrors erected in their back yard. Other than the traumatic burping, tooting, and claustrophobic atmosphere of the interior, I'm sure the juveniles also provided epic full volume screams while playing hose wars, Bloody Murder, and Ghost in the Graveyard. If my offspring had any sense, she would have barricaded herself in the basement with a baby monitor till the whole thing was over. Having camped before, she was surprised how all of a sudden she disliked such shrill-filled accommodations. And thank heaven for Handi-Wipes. A similar kid who had an allergic reaction to water was the same kid who was launching turd torpedos in the toitee. And when you are sleeping in close proximity to other parasites, germs can spread as quickly as a grandmother's behind.

My daughter never got to doze. Not with the presence of spirited nocturnal grazing girlfriends buzzed on candy and freezer treats. With a glazed all-nighter look she asked, "Who wants eggs and toast?" She heard in unison, "Not me!" Then she asked, "How about bagels with cream cheese, or muffins? How about pancakes? I can whip up some awfully wonderful flapjacks." But all she got were blank stares. With the wit she so naturally possesses, she filled a bowl with the remaining Crunch-

N-Munch and declared, "Knock yourselves out! And if you don't hurry and eat it, my mother will be over hogging the bowl, and she may even eat the box!" She told me their eyes bugged out with belief while my granddaughter giggled away. Had she consulted with Parents Magazine on "fifty ways to shut girls up at a sleep-over," feeding them sugary substances for breakfast was not exactly listed as number one.

No one really wrote an article like that, but maybe somebody should have. I suppose sending kiddies home full of sucrose was partial punishment for not getting any sleep herself. Or for having to sit with those girls left behind whose parents didn't bother to pick them up on time. With that hour-and-a-half delay, she still had time to load the kids up on sugar cubes. But my exemplary daughter made the best of it by having a chalk contest on the driveway. I'm surprised she didn't draw a dead body outline with the no-show parents' names inside of it.

Doctors Do-Little

I had a gynecologist once who quite frankly, did not pass the family planning part of obstetrics when my firstborn was two weeks and seventeen hours overdue. Nor was he good at gender determination. He predicted a boy. Three times. Now I have a closet full of Tonka trucks and coveralls in blue.

Come to think of it, this was the same licensed butcher who made me believe that a Cesarean section was a region in Rome. I was at the point of feeling like all doctors inhabiting our glorious globe are characters of intrinsic gloom. When they are done with me, I either need a hug, or fifteen shots of Chambord. They prescribe dinosaur capsules, which I will obediently force down my esophagus once they pulverize them into pieces the size of ice cream sprinkles, and they taste like ice cream sprinkles. I start experiencing impatience and wrist problems just getting the caps off prescription bottles. Then they want you to take the medication every day until they come up with another cure. I'll probably find out that arugula is fattening and aspirin is extremely fatal for me. How precise is the Hippo-critical Oath when healthcare professionals swear upon healing gods to uphold specific standards? Yet they are never at their specific office at the specified time that I've made my appointment, nor are they capable of curing me. They can't even detect problems when they are as obvious as severed limbs and shotgun wounds. Not to mention they charge enough to buy themselves luxurious yachts. The only doctors who have served me well are Dr. Scholl and

Doc Martens.

Back when I had my first two children, it was a day like any other day, with plenty of sunshine headed my way until I went to the doctor. I started walking around work like a drunken soldier-ess, so I went to see a general practitioner. It petrified me knowing he would make me gag for the trillionth time with a throat stick. What worried me more was seeing this man's office filled with archaic types of forceps and literature on bloodletting, which is the ancient practitioner's belief that sickness was merely the result of bad blood. My doctor's diagnosis, or should I say flippant guesstimation, was that I had a brain tumor. My mind was wobbling with the idea of two things. First, I'm going to die, so who will care for my children? Secondly, the big buffoon should really trim back his beard and hide his hemorrhoidal hot iron. Both were about as likely as catching Larry Flynt reading the Bible. My first reaction to this news reached gasping proportions. Now I'm no symptomatic genius, but something else told me that my equilibrium was simply off.

I cried all the way home the day I got that wonderful evaluation. When you think about it, a mother usually sobs during sad movies, when her children are hurt, or when she's out of wine. She shouldn't be crying over the idea of impending termination. I would have probably gotten a brighter forecast if I charted astrologically what was really in store for me or simply gone to a palm reader. Doctor Death put me on a treatment treadmill by prescribing enough pills to put me out permanently. After two weeks of stumbling around from the medications that caused even more dizziness, I resorted to my own remedy by quitting the pills completely, and all my symptoms disappeared. I wanted to go back to the mighty

MD repeating the lyrics of Robert Palmer. "Doctor, doctor, what's with that news? Now I've got a case of loathing you!" He repaid me the kind pleasure of pretending to know who I was.

It just goes to show that by using my own self awareness, intuitive healing, and natural remedy, I too can be certified by a Medical Board of Behavioral Sciences. I'm not any healthier from taking prescribed supplements, just as I'm not any calmer from drinking chamomile teas. After realizing that I wasn't leaving this world quite yet, I did have to tell my children that their next mommy wasn't going to let them have ice cream for dinner either. So they had to be prepared to put up with me awhile longer.

I had to go back to the doctor's office that same week all because my baby picked an unfavorable time to cram a cut carrot up her nose. I paid sixty bucks to have Slim Pickens use his own pair of pliers to pull out the veggie. Although I didn't have to take her to the doctor when she ate a whole box of Cheez-Its and half a box of Teddy Grahams. Instead, I had an emergency treated injury myself after falling onto her Lil' Chef kitchen while flinging myself forward in an attempt to retrieve the packaged goodies from her grip. We all have our own vision of what constitutes fun. It's my every desire to be counting the ceiling tiles in a physician's waiting room, eight hundred times. And it must be every child's desire to sit crying while growing cobwebs, preparing for a man in a white coat to come rescue them and give them a sucker. If nothing else, I've learned that waiting rooms are excellent places to prepare for insane asylums.

I often wondered what other prominent doctors would have done had I gone to them with my initial symptom. I'm convinced that Dr. Heathcliff Huxtable would have told a joke and let laughter be his best medicine. Doogie Howser would have sung to me, "The neck bone's connected to the head bone." Surly Ben Casey would have said, "Darn it, Patty, I'm a doctor. Not a miracle worker!" And Hawkeye Pierce would have told me that there's nothing that can't be cured without a martini and a pair of hedge trimmers.

The Other Woman

Recently I scanned a complete manual of things that might kill you. Listed was a stack of trappings that included ovarian cancer, fairground accidents, eating apples from a manchineel tree, and having a mother-in-law. Just kidding. But most of the time when someone wants an unsolicited opinion, they can get it from the reluctantly related woman who has given birth to your husband. And if there are children involved, some say that co-parenting with a sociopathic troublemaker is a special kind of hell where you are constantly thinking up a viable exit strategy. I was one of the lucky ones. Mine would never have been cast for the movie Monster-in-Law since she was not manipulative or vindictive in any way. I was worried though, when they had just named a hurricane after her.

Lemoncholy was probably the word that most described how I felt about partnering with this lady, which left me downing a coupla citrusy Arnold Palmers that facilitated some deep concerns about sharing my husband. And I felt the intense pressure to produce offspring when she was around. Maybe it was the cutout magazine ads for Gerber. Or the fact that she watched me draw and paint pictures when I should be nursing or diapering. I felt her silent stares one day as if she were to say, "Now walk away from that artist's easel, and go start making me some grandchildren." So I did, after she went home of course. It wasn't long before she was one happy lady who held onto my postpartum belly for nine months and showed up in the delivery room ready to grab my daughter the second she slid out of the birth canal. But that was okay since I couldn't get up or anything, and the man I married was gravitationally challenged and basically needed smelling salts. That was a good bonding experience, especially after she viewed my privates. Then I was twice blessed with having a baby that inherited every last one of my in-laws' traits. My infant didn't look anything like me except for a few eyelashes. It was also an odd coincidence that my kiddo was the spitting image of the hunkish teen who mowed our lawn.

My MIL wanted to get my first baby's ears pierced at the budding age of six months. It may have been a hopeful experience that might have changed my whole attitude towards the usefulness of nose, nipple, and naval rings. But I wanted my teensy tot to be old enough to handle the responsibility of caring for those ears all by herself. My daughter would have probably loved to go bungee jumping as well. But that wasn't going to happen either. My newly kin folk said the piercings could be done by an insightful and caring staff that uses high quality jewelry. If it weren't for my MIL, I would never have known the luxury of owning cashmere. So I wondered if the earrings were coming from Cartier. And if so, I could surely get mine done instead.

Thankfully I didn't have to reach for love potion number ninety-nine when my MIL was around because she was a delightful creature who didn't make me resort to drinking. I didn't get Cartier earrings, nor did my daughter. But she did teach me how to keep my babes away from undetectable poisons or being mauled by unsuspecting characters. She helped me when I had no functioning brain cells after being up all night with feverish and restless children. She supplied plenty of hugs and conversations with my babies in the wee hours of the morning and let me sleep. I couldn't be sad having her around. Not when Pottery Barn should hail her as the reigning queen of tablecloth usage since she let my toddlers run around with my fine Belgian Flax linen that doubled as a tent. She also taught my kids how to dial her phone number. That's why my outlandish phone bills had misdialed charges to foreign countries. But with grandmothers around, toddlers don't ask for an apple, then refuse the apple, then ask why the apple was cut up, then cry because the apple was in wedges instead of cut into giraffe shapes. Kids are just happier people. It was the marriage that turned out not so successful.

Come to find out, there are lots of people out there who are crammed into crowded corners of their own homes jockeying for cabinet positions with a hurricane of troublesome MIL figures. One of my friends commented about the days his smother-in-law visits. I thought she may have been a sea serpent since he always used the phrase, "Thar she blows." His otherwise silent mouthed cries for help are met by the discerning eyes of a woman who supplies a large amount of condescending tutorials. Supposedly she possesses a demeanor that suggests Hitler is in the house, knowing if he acts on his feelings he will either go to prison or be separated from his wife within a matter of minutes. He added that she most resembles a bat whose body is covered with hair and leathery skin. And in order to keep such wildlife under control, he makes a special place in the rafters in the garage where her highness can hang upside down to sleep. He also leaves out lots of almonds and cashews because whatsherface has nut allergies. He calls her a dirtwater fox because her real name often escapes him. But out of respect for his wife, he calls her Duchess.

Now it's my turn to be a mother-in-law. I suspect that any man who treats his woman like a princess is proof that he has been raised by a queenly matriarch. I can only hope for jovial companionship where the jokes are small and the love and laughter are plentiful. But if I go to my son-in-law's house for my birthday, and he has bought me a chair containing straps with electrical wiring and is waiting for me to sit in it so he can plug it in, I'll know something's wrong.

I Got the Music in Me

Anything that contains rhythm, melody, and harmony comforts my soul. When I turn music on, I turn off the world and all is well. However Adelle's rendition of "Someone Like You" reminds me of that vengeful madman who made car contact with me in the fast lane two years ago after I supposedly crossed four feet over the line and cut him off. Technically, it was my road too. He let me down by not watching what I was doing, which was rocking out to oldies.

The pacifying Beatles never let me down after a hard day's night. They can't buy me love, but they sure can settle my weary self eight days a week and make me twist and shout. There are really only seven days in a week, but who's counting when you're being entertained by four hotshot maestros with resplendent singing abilities. Once when I had a cold and was under the influence of NyQuil, listening to their music was more than good mood medicine. Within thirty minutes, I felt like I was a walrus named Jude who was living in a yellow submarine made out of Norwegian wood. And one time when I was severely sleep deprived, I found myself singing to my newborn, "Baby you're a rich man." I'm not sure why when we were living on a very tight salary, and my infant was a girl. And whenever I hear Rocky Raccoon, it makes me want to examine nature and the wilderness by checking myself into the local saloon in some black mountain hill of Dakota. But it might be a big mistake when reading Gideon's Bible may lead to gunplay. Not to mention raccoons can be rabid, and everyone would know me as Nancy.

No matter the situation, music has been the best darn thing since sliced cornbread. I could always get satisfaction listening to the Rolling Stones. As for Jimi Hendrix, I could have had many severely enlightening psychedelic experiences with that man, but I had to have my brain functioning come Monday mornings. Music is my life when I'm happy or sad. I turn up the volume and it's like I'm in a completely different universe until other drivers or my neighbors yell, "Turn that thing down!" As Ella Fitzgerald so passionately puts it, "I got rhythm, I got music, I got my man, who could ask for anything more."

I am constantly reminiscing about the days of old with my fellow Michigander Bob Seger and his good time rock & roll, the kind of music that soothed my soul, but not necessarily the soul of my mother. By 1967, I had already celebrated fourteen years in the music business. My siblings and I used household objects for making sweet music together. My sister played the empty toilet paper roll flute, one brother got into heavy metal and beat the bottom of the kitchen kettle, and I became the brass section by banging a pair of candelabras against whatever furniture was in front of me. Mom said I was a treble maker. I couldn't help it if she was into romance novels and I was into making noise. All I can say is that it was a good thing we didn't own bagpipes or a xylophone. A kid down the street was a hardcore and horrible bassoonist who showed up regularly to assist in the sibling band. Two minutes into it and my saintly mother turned fibber said, "Your Mom called. She wants you home immediately." It was bad enough that we had several sets of lungs in our house let alone that extra disturbance. A younger sibling tried making splendidly creative cymbals out of every one of my dad's records. And one time my musical director brother attempted to lambaste the percussionist with the pastry roller turned wand he was using. The drummer didn't mind swinging his wooden spoons during this commotion since they too doubled as weapons. My mother pledged that day to ban every assault instrument. She said unless we were the Detroit Symphony Orchestra, we should go outside and play. For Mom's birthday one year, her beautiful losers composed a classic musical arrangement and newer version of "Against the Wind" that would go down in making bad music history. It was an event she would never forget.

As a teen, I wanted to be a singer in the worst way. Mom warned me about politicians and musicians. She said if I wasn't careful, men would come along who work out of town a lot and who would possibly leave me for twenty other women who are way more bodylicious than I was. I feared a future alongside some band member, when sheet music might mean doing something on a flat surface like a trailer floor with already soiled bed linens. On a scale from one to whore, my mother pretty much wanted me dating a zero, someone who was super conservative and preferably with some distance between us. Which to her meant sitting in front of the television tube every Saturday night swooning over the wunnerful, wunnerful, Lawrence Welk. He was a nice old music lover, but his ballads creeped me out. Besides, I was hungry for more modern listening enjoyment. Not be tied down to champagne music.

Forty weeks into pregnancy and I was pretty irritable, especially that last excruciating hour. If it wasn't for the mellow sounds of Enya, I would have clawed my husband to death. Then my kids grew into testy teens. I listened to the Ramones with their random acts of helpfulness, when "twenty-twenty-twenty-four hours a day, I wanted to be sedated." I wished my doctor would have prescribed something before I went bonkers, since I couldn't control my kids, and I surely couldn't control my brain. I felt like Mary Travers since my bags were packed and ready to go. I wanted somebody to put me on a jet plane not knowing if I'd ever be back again. My youngest daughter hated it when I sang in the car, or anywhere else. Sometimes I'd say, "It's mic-and-cheese night. Wanna join me?" She wanted the number for Pizza Hut. After thinking it through, I shrugged off everything she ever said to me about my singing. Sometimes I greeted her at the school steps singing soprano or acapella. Of course she didn't like it very much when I was performing, "I got the sneering, cranky, and uptight kid blues."

God knows I've listened to music many times while I've been slightly inebriated. I couldn't find Funkytown on the globe, or Mapquest. I've also been prone to sudden outbursts of karaoke, howling, "O K L A H O M A, where the wind comes sweepin' down the plain." It's long been a tradition in karaoke to project the best we can. I hardly even noticed the instant feedback of booing. But when I'm feeling like a superstar, it's kinda hard stopping my shine. I felt as accomplished as I did the time I skied into a tree. The next song went out to the boy who stole my heart and dumped me for that lanky brunette back in ninth grade.

Even sober, I engage in voluntary explosion of the lungs. Last year I sounded like Bing Crosby when I belted out, "I'm dreaming of a crystal Christmas." I still sing in the car, during dental visits, and I'm extremely fun at baby showers.

Somewhere in my Wicked Parenting Past, I Must Have Done Something Good

When the Lord closes a door, He opens regrets. Because somewhere in my supposedly wicked child rearing, there were many moments of apprehension when I couldn't buy ponies for my kids. There they were, standing there, hating me. But I figured foal can be just as stubborn as children. Eight hundred pounds of dense bone and manure smelling Equidae eating me out of house and lawn was too much compared to goldfish. I was equally remorseful when I couldn't get them a unicorn or a Pegasus.

There are many things I would do differently if I was brave and young enough to have another child. First of all, I would need to have more things in common with Maria von Trapp. Sounds of music and good vocals, unique ability to solve problems and sew clothes from heavy drapery material, postulancy for entering an abbey when things went haywire at home. I would have a surrogate so I wasn't left with belly marks that stretch from here to Hungary. I also have to say that making room for ponies in the house would have saved me from scowls. And a cow sure would have made nursing simpler. All I would need to do is slip my babies underneath some udders, and the sucklings could feed all day while I did other things. It is a known fact that if you nipple feed, infants become dependent and eventually demand cell phones and expensive clothing.

Dysphoria filled my house along with toddler temperaments, something I never saw coming. How timid and shy and scared I was when my inquisitive little ones decided to climb every mountainous cabinet in the kitchen looking for Fruit Loops, then ford through every ice cream container that left melted dairy on my fabric chairs. Of course eating at the same time they were applying glitter nail polish. I would never again turn my head for two seconds and have a tot teetering trying to get into the freezer, turning on the filled blender without a lid, or have adorable dance-offs on table tops. My youngest child was so cute, until I found cupcakes that I baked for a birthday party in brown paper packages tied up with every last bit of decorative stringy dental floss and was gifting them to the neighbor kids. Plus, far was a long, long way to run when my second cherub left drops of golden sun, or rather tinkling rain, all over the carpeting. A few of my favorite things did not include having my eldest toddler trying to make concrete by pouring a whole box of powdered detergent into the dishwasher. I would certainly take my younguns to McDonald's Playplace way more often. The best moments in life are kids filled with crappy meals and being exposed to germy jungle gyms, which would surely help boost their immune systems.

 Such upheaval lies in households when children are involved. This pearl of wisdom came after hearing my own parents' loud shouts about community property and threatening divorce. I was so shaken until I realized they were playing Monopoly. I suppose I was full of indignation. I regret not responding more appropriately when questioned, "Is it to be at every meal, or merely at dinnertime, that you intend on leading us all through this rare and wonderful new world of... indigestion?" If they had their second chances, I wonder if they would have had us. They were probably drinking pure vodka with their jam and bread.

My girls never pulled whiskers on kittens. But at one point, one of my lovelies left my bright copper kettle disastrously charred by leaving it on the stove. I wouldn't call chlorine the most sweet-smelling of all aromas. But it sure switched black socks into fifty shades of gray when unproperly washed by my energetically bleach-minded adolescents. I should have installed surveillance cameras to see everything my sixteen-going-on-seventeeners were doing. It would be truly entertaining now to see a teenager on film washing the collie in the bathroom using a squirt bottle and Soft Scrub. I would have liked to be watching them more carefully to make absolutely sure the boys they entertained weren't Nazi sympathizers. And I would chime "Nothing comes from nothing" when talking to them about sex. I wouldn't want to fall on the human cruelty scale when eyeing them more closely, or when taking away privileges. So during a momentary lull in hostile takeovers, I'd soothe the situation by gathering my offspring together to sound out "supercalifragilisticexpialidocious." Okay, that was Mary Poppins. Maybe I would adopt some of her nanny-ish characteristics as well.

My second chance at mothering would include saving every last pre-school and kindergarten project my children ever made. Hell hath no fury like females who find their inventive artwork wilting underneath cantaloupe innards in the kitchen garbage. One of my daughters thought a huge rope necklace would look good on me. I would have saved it if I'd known later on that I needed a noose. I'd make the decision to home school then bring in a competent nanny to teach my youngsters a thing or two. Going to school requires bathing and brushing teeth, so

I wouldn't sound so psycho trying to get through habits of hygiene and pushing them off to the bus most mornings. I'd also have Humpty Dumpty themed parties and have all the attendees fetch me pails of wine. You can't tell me Maria didn't indulge in something herself while trying to survive turmoil, besides that Baroness. On the bright side, at least I wasn't addicted to something harsher like heroin. Like Maria, I probably wouldn't have made a very good nun either. But regardless of what I went through, I would emphasize my fondness for each one of my daughters by telling people, "She's a headache, she's an angel, she's a girl."

Since having more children is inconceivably out of the question, there is still time to go to my grown girl's homes. There's many a thing I know I'd like to tell them, and many a thing they ought to understand when I open their freezer door twenty times, climb on their countertops, chug some chocolate syrup, scribble on their walls, pour chlorine on their colored clothes, interrupt them incessantly, whine, and moan at their messes. They'll completely get it when I walk away singing, "So long, farewell, auf Wiedersehen, good night! I'm going home and leave your pretty sights!" I'm sure their hearts will want to "sigh like a chime that flies from a church, on a breeze."

Wash today—or naked tomorrow!

Will Work for Socks

It's been the American horror story, that paranormal activity within laundry rooms on those solemn occasions when socks come up missing. I have owned about four thousand elastic hair bands in my lifetime, and guess how many I have now? Not counting the ones our elastic fetished feline vomited up or flung with her paws into oblivion. No one wants to sense the slow agonizing fury of departure. Socks are no different.

If you've been lucky enough to go to your dryer and pull out matching sole mates, then you're doing far better than most people. There might be hundreds who have their heads bowed in prayerful appreciation when their foot wrapping comes out of dry rotation with its twin. I am in awe of the few, the proud, the machines that consistently pop out pairs. I helped my mother with laundering, and that was never the case. She interrupted my playtime to tell me it was hunting season, like I was suppose be socktually stimulated and turn into a footsie wear detective...as if it was an attempt to associate me with another behavioral trait of carelessness.

I wondered if this is how the phrase "sock it to me" originated. Chances were that the socks wound up pasted to the washer or dryer drum during their whirl or were suctioned inside a trouser leg. If missing socks didn't resurface within the first five minutes, the recovery rate would therefore be slim to zero. Mom would be mourning the losses then go broke buying more. I suspected that they were abducted by aliens or sibling hand puppeteers. Or by brothers who used them as dog

dickeys.
Mom originally delegated this daunting dryer task to me. Then after many missing socks, demoted me to grimy laundry washing. There was something always to be said about dirty socks. My siblings would saunter into the laundry room after trailing through the grungy pumice paths of outside soil, or doing risky business Tom Cruise style sliding on unwashed floors. You could tell by the flex of their feet that I wasn't orgasmic. I was never one to condone a hot n' sweaty socks scene, although I didn't care who died in them as long as I didn't have to remove them from the bodies and place them in the washing machine. If cringing was a color, it would be dismal smelly brown.

I don't know how my mother ever did keep track of ten children and socks. The puzzlement continued when I had kids of my own and came to the conclusion that I owned both washer and spin cycling knitivores. Socks were eaten then somehow mysteriously disappeared into nowhere. Today it is trendy to wear mismatched socks. How I wish it was that way when I was on a mission to send my kids off to school in paired footwear, only to find out that I walked to the bus stop with my shirt on inside out. I was equally unfashionable wearing socks with flip flops.

Living in Michigan part of my life, I had foot mittens made from virgin wool. Opposed to what? Socks made from promiscuous sheep? Now I'm not one to tout the virtues of certain fiber material. But no itch, no bitch. I prefer cotton over wool. And polyester. And nylon. Acrylics should be reserved for painting. If mine were merino, I would appear spasmodic with bouts of severe scratching. I embodied enough genetic material to constitute the genome of a woolly mammoth living in the permafrostic ice age. I'm sure those animals became extinct because they had too much fleece in their pathway of procreating. I wore any kinds of knee socks so I wouldn't have to shave the jungle on my legs. Of course with it came the worst cases of staticshockophobia when I wore socks that were not rinsed with fabric softeners. I only wish I'd been the one to invent dryer sheets first. All I needed to do was throw a bunch of mints into socks, coat them with hair conditioner, tie them up, and I'd be making millions as well.

I swore I would never date a man who wore socks to bed. Luckily that's all my boyfriend wears. I wear them myself whenever I have unsexy chipped nail polish and haven't had time to get a pedicure. I can never have enough warmth for my tootsies. And it sure helps to have socks for traction when you're slipping and sliding around on satin sheets. Who knows if Hanes will make them my way and come out with Cheetah prints for the most masculine of men. There's nothing sexier than seeing Deedle Deedle Dumpling in a pair of bestial prints, bringing out the total animal in him. Hopefully he will never get cold feet. My husband owned a variety of socks for different days. I always knew which pair was for golfing because of the hole in one. He bought crimson colored low cuts which totally spelled eroticism. Although the mood lessened after I noticed "Red Sox" printed on them.

It takes a lot of hard earned paychecks to stay supplied with those important things in life like food, socks, and hair bands. In the interest of sock safety, washers and dryers should have their own tracking system. I did have the brainstorm of opening a Sockorama, for those whose fallen comrades have flown the proverbial laundry coop. I figured it is my patriotic duty to provide a system where you can drop off your onesies and pick up a pair for free. Either that, or start a California Sock Exchange and offer crazy days of trading.

Estrogen-arian Allies

"I still find each day too short for all the thoughts I want to think, all the walks I want to take, all the books I want to read, and all the friends I want to see."
- John Burroughs

My friendly playmates and I understand that in times of desperation, friends don't let friends drive over a cliff. Plus calling each other 77,000 times a week does not imply stalking. It just means we have to tell each other something. Badly. We have often thought about a Golden Girls scenario where we'll spend the rest of human eternity under one roof engaging in some high-spirited shenanigans. We like referring to each other as desirous seasoned hussies. The moment you realize most of your friends share the same debauched sense of humor, you're not exactly sure whether to be pleased or petrified.

Here's the thing about girlfriends. You can rely on them to carry a pursed inventory of mints, moisturizers, Macy's coupons, personal pan pizzas, flasks, and keys to a hidden hideaway if you need a place to flee. If you go shopping together, they will carefully examine sizes and styles as if they are border inspectors. They will safeguard you with persuasive mammogram screenings, promising that they won't turn your boobies into radioactive beaver tails. I went more willingly after a friend bribed me with lunch. If she treated to breakfasts, dinners, or Prada pumps, I'd get mammograms a lot more often. We have never questioned why we weren't born boys. We like being the delicate flowers that we are. What we don't like is the wilting and drying out.

My gal pals make me colorful cocktails and relish the opportunity to hold mine while they distract me. They have stood by me through thick and thinning hair, and I love the fact that I can tell the same story five times and they will switch conversations carefully so I don't look like a real stupe. We've never been into mind games, although words frequently forgotten may force me to act them out by playing Charades. Life doesn't always supply us with every amusement, so we invent new ones. But I admit, I am a terrible phone conversationalist. It's probably the only time I give someone the silent treatment. My friendships have been built on the firm foundation of loyalty and the talk of one day getting physically active. We aren't the world's most watchful calorie counters. I come from a long friendship line of bakery loving beauties who continue to avoid opportunities to bench press. It's not their fault that they bypass the gym and end up at Costco, and go home with extra large containers of pastries. Eating at their homes is like eating at a large town buffet. I never go home hungry. Or thirsty. Not that healthiness doesn't run in my circle of chums, nobody runs in my circle of chums. I find myself paraphrasing Sinatra when it comes to my friends and the foods they prepare. "I've got you and your hydrogenates under my skin." My body isn't naturally this glowing all over. Pounds of shortening have made me this way.

We all have our vices. Without concealing names, I'll give you a slight character portrait of my pals. Virgo taught me that tire irons have many uses. Leo says size does matter when it comes to Mai-Tai's. Gemini is extremely rich with platinum teeth, her copper tan, and lead feet. Pisces believes that extreme shopping is not a mental illness and that everyone needs to buy four outfits per day. Scorpio is always late, but worth the wait. The IRS may not put up with her, but I do. She's got this theory that it's better to be late than to arrive looking awful. Then there's Libra. Every cell of her saintliness can become Rambo rigorous and raring to take on someone who crosses me. Sagittarius shares this idealized image of us atop shiny mares riding away from all evils. Although we will probably end up horse thrown and burning somewhere in the afterlife. Taurus can get suicidal, and her mood depends on where she is in her life cycle. If she's slim, she's ecstatic. If she's the slightest bit overweight, well... just picture Goddess-zilla.

I have my worries about new friends. Heaven forbid if I invite them for drinks and dinner and they have peanut butter sandwich allergies. Hopefully they will still like me after the allergic reaction. It would be my greatest last dying wish to say, "I'm leaving you my finest china hidden under the..." and sincerely hope I don't croak before compensating them. I make friends fairly easily, with certain exceptions. I was at a dueling pianos eatery when I asked the darling insightful teen waitress and possible future friend of mine what a hanger steak was, which I found out later is a cut of beef prized for its flavor and derived from the diaphragm of a steer. This girl told me, "Geez lady, it comes from a cow." Not to mention she got my drink order totally wrong by bringing me a very little liquor filled martini with a lime instead of my usual 99% vodka with five cherries. I had this feeling, woohoo, that the night was going to be a good, good but long night. I quickly summed up that I had enough children—er, friends—in my life.

I value one lady friend who is eighty-two years young

and an absolute charm. She phoned to inform me that she has a terminal condition. I froze. But then I heard, "The condition is called old age." She must have giggled for three solid minutes. To all the females now that I adore, I'm so glad your parents were also reckless with birth control. And thanks for keeping an array of precious cargo in your purses. I hold a special place for you in my heart about half a millimeter away from my pulmonary valve. We'll be friends till we are senile, then I suggest we wear friendship bracelets to remind us that we are friends.

Hello, Anyone Home?

I've been out to lunch. No, really out to lunch. In the atmosphere, spacing out, oblivious, eradicating the world around me. In fact I have given in to many bouts of this behavior and have fallen prey to the immeasurable charms of scatterbrainism. It doesn't take mind altering substances to arrive at this mental wandering. I am noticing more and more people with the same disease, much like Sigmund Freud's beliefs and theories that the unconscious mind takes exception with the ideas of the conscious resulting in conflicting attitudes. Even some Einstein images suggest a person detached from the universe.

It began with childbirth. So I'd like to tell you what really goes on after an epidural. The numbing medicine wouldn't take and I thought I was stuck going natural. One instance showed my digressive behavior flaring with satirical thrusts thrown at family members. Everyone was panning the better part of my laboring shindig, hovering over my draped yet naked bottom half which wasn't exactly there for anyone's placenta viewing pleasure. When my baby proved late for the premier, everyone's eyes were peeled to my cervical dilation. Capricious me was overdramatizing the whole situation when my seriously fatigued self couldn't push a watermelon out of a pea-sized opening. I wasn't getting a groundswell of sympathy, although my husband could totally relate to my pain when he had the sniffles the week before. All that pushing undoubtedly put pressure on my brain.

It turned to a joyous experience once the epidural took. It felt like ten warm beers had been injected through the needle. I was hungry to boot after seeing the doctor use forceps that I thought were salad tongs. Asian apple slaw is one of the things you do think about while groaning a newborn out of you. I was playing Charades with the nurses when I noticed heavy rain outside the window, so I consecrated the wet downfall with the sign of the cross. Apparently I blessed the rains down in Africa too. Then I turned to Dr. McDreamy asking if he wanted to do the ballroom rumba. He said it looked as though I had already done the bedroom rumba and that's how I ended up in that situation to begin with. I learned never to hire a good looking physician to come calling when your head is covered in rollers and undergarments aren't exactly optional. I also shouldn't have let him see my un-spa'd nails that I was totally on my to-do list, which was also right there next to GIVE BIRTH. Not to mention handing over my purse to a hair color rapist so I would look horizontally gorgeous for the cast and crew of *General Hospital*.

As time went on, I was continuously reminded of my blunders regardless of whether or not I was under the influence of anything. Truly? I don't think the epidural ever left my system. Like the time I wore a multitinted T-shirt to Walmart. I was pulled over by the manager who asked me to be their paint mixer. To my knowledge, this had never happened before. Although he was used to seeing freakish women with horrible hair, ratty sweats, and paint splatters on clothes and embedded under fingernails. I should have taken him up on his offer and become a useful soul in society. Instead, I went to work at a Bed and Breakfast where one day before work, I took a Tylenol and popped a Tylenol PM by mistake. An hour later I was asleep at the desk. People walked in for continental breakfast and thought I was dead. Not to mention I was brain mush for the rest of my shift. I stood a better chance of being a spokeswoman for Sealy mattresses. I tried drinking coffee and energy drinks, and didn't sleep for three days. In other bouts of brainlessness, I have brushed my teeth with Polysporin, washed my hair with conditioner, and put plates in the fridge and milk in the medicine cabinet. Now I spend much of my sprightly remaining time on earth going to the grocer's for milk and searching the dairy department for a cow.

My youngest daughter used to think I was wacko material just because I cut her off mid-sentence when she was snarling about something trivial. Since anything I said would be held against me anyway, I was inclined to muster up something like Gene Chandler's "Duke, Duke, Duke, Duke of Earl Duke Duke." She looked at me as if the *Battlestar Gallactica* just landed in the living room and out I stepped. Then she'd ask who the heck Duke of Earl was. She also asked me if I knew who The Rolling Stones were. Sometimes you just have to sing "Gimme Shelter" to jog their musical memory a bit. I wanted to say "duh," followed by a ghastly lip curl that translates into "geez, don't you know anything??" But I didn't. It would have just widened the disconnect that was going on between mother and teenage daughter. Instead, I poured myself a martini. I had houseplants galore, but couldn't smoke any of them.

Like paranormalist Uri Gellar believes, maybe I too came from the distant planet of Hoova. My concerned offspring already wanted to invest in some drill bits so she could tighten my so-called loose screws. Suffice to say, she's inheriting my humoristic personality. At one point she sat next to me observing my changing chassis and belted out, "Your boobs are starting to sag." The comedienne started singing, "Do your boobs hang low, do they wobble to and fro, can you tie them in a knot, can you tie them in a bow, can you throw them over your shoulder, since you've gotten so much older, is this what I have to look forward to because I'll schedule my reconstructive surgery right now fa la la la la, la la la la!??" I had to wail with laughter knowing girls just wanna have fun at any age.

We've all been there when life gets cobwebby, and have done things that were absentmindedly stupid. When I was a new mother, my sterilizer broke and I had to boil baby bottle nipples the medieval way. I walked away and failed to tie a timer to my earlobe. I remembered them when burning rubber and a charred pan caught my nostrils attention. Old habits die hard. One day while driving I decided to make a courtesy call to an elderly friend. I got caught up in her diarrhea disaster, passing my exit and ending up in Timbuktu. I have also put a pot roast in and turned the oven on broil. Although I'm pretty sure when I'm dead I won't be turned away from the Kingdom for inadvertently killing cookware. I confessed to a friend who said, "Don't fret you marvelous vintage vessel, I've done that too! I think it also happened to almost everyone on *Dallas* including J.R. and Sue Ellen's second cousin."

I asked if it was her second cousin once removed.

Some people just know what to say to make you feel better. As I woefully admit, it isn't going to improve. I just want to get through my mornings without spilling my coffee on my keyboard while self-manicuring and talking on the phone, let alone do dumb things. Nobel winner Rabindranath Tagore profoundly said, "The burden of self is lightened when I can laugh at myself." I can only hope I am never listed in the Dodo Directory or nominated for the Darwin Awards.

Lovin' Spoonfuls

Young parents these days are a bit more attentive to pesticides, additives, and preservatives than my generation was. Having become a grandmother my second time around, I can't help but ponder the practices of child sustenance and what awaits this new mother. I'm surprised the food industry hasn't come out with low fat tofu Tater Tots.

In my day, women didn't nurse in public, simply because you couldn't subject engorged weapons of lump filled lactation without stares of indecent exposure. My middle daughter pretty much rejected my colostrum anyway after realizing it wasn't chocolate milk. However, it was my passion to put a twinkle in my starling's eyes by pleasing her palate. Her year-old mumbling voice clamored for my cuisinely challenged attentiveness, trying to divert me down the path of confections. We had to come up with a mutually beneficial plan for her happiness. Guiding me was Dr. Spock, although he prophesied that there are only two things a child will share voluntarily. Communicable diseases and its mother's age.

While I worried about my daughter's fuel deficiencies, Kix was meanwhile kid tested and mother approved. I used the old spoon/airplane technique trying to land un-sweetened cereal past her lips. She scoffed, probably fearing that I would forge the tasteless ramjet down her esophagus. Before long I became a punster air pilot professional. I tried everything from oatmeal to lima beans sprinkled with cinnamon. Sometimes I threw her a hot dog, and she willingly ate it as long as I made smiley faces with ketchup on her plate, put a bendy straw in her drinks, took away the bun, chopped the meat into microscopic pieces, and spoon fed them with an ice cream scooper layered with ice cream.

One time I had an early morning power outage. The big thaw forced me to feed her fish filets, chicken cutlets, ground beef, and mushy mixed vegetables for breakfast. For she was a jolly good food-flinger, and I came precariously close to having a fist flung in my face. I should have worn a crash helmet while waving a white flag. The only way to minimize sorrow that came with every eating experience was through sugar. But that wasn't listed in Spock's advisories. Look who she had as a role model. Me. The queen of sweets. Children who aren't allowed much sugar growing up subsequently end up siphoning anything that contains sucrose.

And nobody doesn't like Sara Lee. Admittedly, I wanted to let there be peace on earth and let it begin with one of her goodies, and let me sit with my toddler in perfect harmony. Except there was a lot more joy in sweet potatoes topped with Chips Ahoy. Though tempered chocolate always discolored my dining room wallpaper. M&M's weren't the only things that melted in places and not in her hands. How many other mothers have had persevering thoughts of piling chocolate morsels or gummy bears on top of broccoli spears? My ankle clinger never wanted to attend school because they force fed her carrots—when I force fed her carrots covered in brown sugar. I'm surprised the two of us haven't developed diabetes.

My cherub loved toast, just not the brown parts. The bread couldn't be wheat or rye or pumpernickel, and the cat had to eat it first. She would happily consume yogurt as long as I called it pudding. Lucky Charms were magically delicious as well if smothered in Hershey's syrup. And she was more likely to eat peas if they were splashed with honey and tossed onto linoleum. That is after she stared at them, poked them, and smashed several onto her chest. I can't wait for the day my daughter tells me her own youngster looks like a chicken-poxed-pea-farmer.

I found out OJ wasn't just for breakfast anymore. It was for anytime I didn't want to see concentrated pulpy extract seeping into my shag carpeting. My little lamb spilled the juice then shot me sober glances while I rattled the ice cubes in my glass filled with lonely vodka. And while choosy mothers may choose Jif, others may choose something entirely different after they've seen peanut butter finger painted on their drapes. I should have given her a side order of acrylics. And supposedly cook's who knew trusted Crisco. I didn't trust it in the hands or mouth of my babe. She didn't need kids at school saying, "Fatty, fatty, two-by-four, can't get through the classroom door." I was already calling her "Sugar Pie, Honey Bunch."

I couldn't screw up grilled cheese. But cheese gave this girl gassiness. In the often occurrences of accidental anal releases, masks did not drop down from little trap doors in the ceiling. I almost lost consciousness from the flotation of rancid air. Once she caught wind of it herself, it was amusing to see the smirks on her face when she said she was blowing me butt kisses. My cutie was a keeper, even though she removed her diaper and left doo doo dumplings on my area rug. I took on the role as her personal pooper scooper. How could I be startlingly disappointed by such progressive and generous company? It would have been worse if she had been a constipated dairy carrier. Equally menacing were the uh oh, Spaghettios. Diabetic retinopathy had risen after my eyes had images of my youngster eating circular saucy shapes from the floor. Visualizing an army of bacterial critters patrolling her body made my own skin crawl. But my daughter came hungry and left healthy and happy.

My home was clearly a Build-a-Babe workshop. I couldn't find one book that would help me contrive new ways to stuff good nutrition into my child. She could never guarantee that she'd eat anything wholesome any more than I could guarantee giving her a unicorn. But when my munchkin woke each morning, I figured I was successful at keeping her alive. And I must say, it is truly satisfying now to see my children grown and not shooting straws full of milk at me while we are dining together.

Clear and Present Wager

A wager is an agreement between two parties in which the one who has made an incorrect prediction about an uncertain outcome will forfeit something stipulated to the other. My boyfriend and I often participate in this kind of competitive challenge. He makes bets with me that I too won't be able to find his glasses when they come up missing. It's like making a wager with a female squirrel that she won't find a nut. As of now, all bets are off. Particularly since he likes to be right, and my money is usually on me. Besides, he likes to bet for sex when I like to bet for things like expensive automobiles and dinners in provinces of France. Thus far, he's been winning the better part of our bets. Not that I object to his favorable winning requests. I'd just be more inclined to grant his wishes in a Porsche or somewhere in the Cote d'Azur.

As ridiculous as my wagers are, I have to simply assume that he came out of school knowing absolutely everything, and he will huff and puff and blow my hypothesis down. Obviously he is the second most competitive mortal I know. Having found the seemingly perfect person to share my life with, it's still a game of he said she said. And being the trail blazers that we are, we bet on who should sit in the driver's seat, who should sit on the passenger side, and who should actually be duct taped at the mouth and riding in the trunk. He wouldn't want it to be him. I go over speed bumps too fast. We do agree that I'm a much better parker, while he is much better at seeing stop signs. However he often puts me in the hot seat where I am steeped in the most pedantic details of a subject matter. Once we faced off on aquafarming and the problems of unsustainable fishing. First of all, he had a clear advantage over me. He knows sports. And he's a fisherman. Now I am smarter than the average reddish-blonde bear. But I'm thinking, how complex can fishing be? You need a rod, beer, boat, body of water, a few fish, and an alluring hooker on board.

My steady opponent went into descriptive statistics and started explaining the economics of fisheries. "Close your eyes and picture all this. Don't you see?" To be honest, I didn't see anything but complete and imperforate darkness underneath my eyelids. I bet him that the only way we will really know that the economy is in bad shape is when Ellen DeGeneres starts giving away Slinkies. Since redirecting conversations is one of my finer attributes, I bet him lunch that he wouldn't know who Gary Oldman is. Which to me is a profound sadness on behalf of filmmaking humanity. But my sweetheart doesn't like to be distracted while driving. I uttered, "Switch places, would ya. I've got a Taco Bell burrito riding on this."

We make bets that there's a right way and a wrong way to eat sushi. I order a fork first. I tried pulling a pair of chopsticks apart and rubbed them together to remove any splinters. My sushiologist hunny bunny indicated that a good sushi bar and grill would never offer splintery sticks. Then he asked me if I was getting prepared to knit a sweater or start a fire. While attempting to pick up a crab roll, I watched all but three grains of rice fall back onto my plate. My disputing dining mate bet me to use chopsticks the next time we went for spaghetti. I preferred to picture us nuzzling over a plate of noodles without any utensils, like Lady and the Tramp. I then bet him to tell the waiter "I'll have what she's having" and make a scene by seductively faking an orgasm.

Meanwhile, the eight-year-old at the next table had already mastered his chopsticking skills while his parents were dining on stir fry. The cat in the sushi hat comes back to inform me that I'm not holding my sticks correctly then walked over to the next table inquiring how their sauteed pork tasted. Whereas he promptly started singing in a strong Japanese accent, "We will, we will wok yoo." I bet my beau that the guy must have gone to some cooking school of the performing arts with Queen. We leaned over to comment to the couple about the singing and they commented on our betting. The wife who looked like she was ready to burst at the seams stated, "I bet my husband that I wouldn't get pregnant. It's been nine months since my last period!"

My man wagered that there would be no wine left in our bottle by the time we were done with dinner. He's always right. Then again when I don't check, he distracts me while siphoning the last few ounces. We went to pay our bill betting that the restaurant would charge us for extra eel sauce. I lost three bets that night, plus my fair share of the wine.

My competitive nature kicked in when I recently bet my boyfriend that Pillsbury cake mix is way more moist than Betty Crocker. I made both, but added a lot more oil to Pillsbury's batter. He wondered why it was greasy and kept slipping off his fork. But I have to confess. I was out to win, risking damnation and possibly poor digestion. I plead guilty and earnestly petitioned for a light sentence upon the grounds of extenuating circumstances. I was born to fool. If I could just win more often I wouldn't have to resort to such trickery. But I figure it this way. Under the law of averages, every time he's able to find the humor in anything I do, I'm a winner.

It's a good thing neither of us want to go to Vegas, that advanced state of agitation. I do know a bet I will always win. I can ask him if he's naked underneath his clothes. But I must say, we adore way more than we annoy each other. That's why we've lasted this long.

Planet of the Grapes

I keep a sign on my front door that says, "No soliciting... unless you're bringing in a bottle of wine and are willing to wash some floors." That sign sits alongside another sign of special importance. "Property protected by a wine swigging female. Boyfriend and parrot may not be upstanding either."

I'm not the only person on the planet with the commonality of such fruitful undertakings as drinking wine. It's sometimes difficult persevering along this life path, which is also fortuitously timed with long hours of employment, uncivilized motorists, government idiocy, and gopher holes in the yard. There are days when we need that second glass, and days we need that second bottle. Although that second bottle should never serve as an inspiration to call Iran in a rather impulsive attempt to cease conflict. Vino may not solve all my problems, but neither will Sake or Tang. I drink because without it, I'm not as good a belly dancer or hula hooper unless I've successfully installed Sauvignon into my system. Sweet dreams are made of these, and I have definitely found my sleep number in glasses of the liquid goodness.

It wasn't until later in life that I started grape cleansing again. I stopped way back when I drank something so sparkling that I scarcely noticed that it was cheap half-concord Cold Duck. I scored high on the popularity poll when I woke with my head spinnin' and a regurgitating tummy. At the time, I believed that I would be a much better individual if I was inebriated. But I didn't know the protocol for this particular amusement.

Nowadays, I like grapes that have been stomped on until they mature into something I'd like to have dinner with and won't make me walk away from feeling so pukey. Three goblets and I was slurring words and dizzily casting off the shackles of normal behavior. My idea of a happy meal was Two-Buck Chuck and a plate of Oreos. As anyone who has had a few with lunch can attest, funny things happen when we're tanked and hyped up on sugar. Picture Gidget in shorty shorts with chocolate crumbed lips, pole dancing on a tree trunk. While I didn't die directly from ethylene glycol additives, I did end up in a state of headache shock. Cheap wines have also chased away other dedicated practitioners.

When I was dating, I practically auditioned men with "Must Love Wine." Only they had to stay sober designated drivers while I proceeded to have all the fun. If guys showed up on first dates insinuating a booty call, I HAD to drink. Once I had kids, I needed to function on all cylinders. So I gave up a career to be a stay-at-home Chianti guzzler. It was the only thing that got me through those years of chaos. One time I think I made the mistake of adding wine to cupcake batter instead of water. My child was in an awfully good mood that day, but turned into a persevering graffiti vandal by placing crayoned sticky notes all over every inch of the house when her younger sister simply passed out. I've spent a significant amount of time in the wine section of the grocer's determining which vintage was the most sedative. My mother was always tethered to a wine glass. I can only imagine her horror when I was her kid who decorated the house with my cake frosting fingertips imitating Vincent van Gogh.

After moving to California, I couldn't be threatened by a drought. Nor did I want to limit my happiness to an hour, especially if somebody else was buyin. I discovered my love for wine in a bottle of Amarone and have stayed winsomely cheerful and somewhat sober ever since. And while practicing random acts of wineness, I drink from bottles only because it isn't available by pods. Which is unfortunate when they're slogan could be, "We Deliver, You Drink, We Pick-Up." I don't want to confuse anyone into thinking that over-intoxication is acceptable. The devil is always around to taunt and tempt us into displays of foolishness. I have tried other intoxicants, like the night I discovered piña coladas. I was highly engaged in a heart-to-heart about sun protection until the barman informed me that I should be talking to people instead of small umbrellas. And yet if I gave up the coconut cocktails, I was afraid I might replace them with shot glasses filled with ouzo or grappa.

My challenge now is going to the grocer's where I stand listening to strong opinions about what shoppers think I should be drinking. I'm never sure which bottle to buy. A bazillion of the stoic forms of fermentation stare back at me then blink their codes of silence. I'm always hoping that some extremely knowledgeable connoisseur will come along and fill me in on the incidental details of chemical balancing and what pleases the palate the most. If I choose a bottle of Chablis, then for sure I'm turning into my mother. If I pick the gallon bottle of Chablis, then I'll know I'm my mother. If I buy a basic blend of Champagne varietals in an off-dry sweetly fortified Shiraz, then I'm really an Aussie. I sometimes wonder how a Riesling will pair with a sometimes emotionally fragile female. If it was left to me, these beverages would be served in every public place throughout the country.

Who knows better than the Europeans, with the quality of tannic red grape content they engage in. Surprisingly, the Vatican City populace has pounced on enough graped beauties with the sole intention of intoxication dominating every other country. The enclave of priests and cardinals are enjoying life a whole lot more than we are. I might have to move there. Their local cider seems very innocuous at first, then wham bam you think you're in Amsterdam discussing Dutch rituals. Here, communion consists of a wafer and a sip of wine. In Rome, they offer a carafe and tell you to go find Jesus.

I will defend drinking these violaceous intoxicants until my dying days of Metamucil mixed with Merlot. So I say drink and be at your merriest, for tomorrow we may be aridly entombed from all those global warnings.

I never show up empty hatted.

Brotherly Love

I'm surprised that I am with a man today considering the former odious advances made by certain males, and the fact that I lived with six brothers. Testosterone ruled in our house. They didn't have to do dishes or wash clothes or make beds. The only reason they even came home at night was because they had clean sheets and liked helping themselves to all the refrigerator contents while everyone else was sleeping. I blamed everything on my brothers. Besides, it felt good redirecting the focus of my parental critics.

My sisters and I were saints. Just ask them. Behind every delinquent brother was a substantial amount of pugnaciousness and Soviet style operations. The world needed new leaders who were cunning and resourceful. But I was seriously concerned about their futures heading more towards maximum security. Especially the times they topped the neighbor's trees with toilet paper or used our mutt for dogsledding. They also decided that there needed to be two kegs and about five thousand kids from school at our house while Mom and Dad were away. It resulted in my first hangover. Needless to say, their secret was safe with me. That night, between trying to sleep and noticing my unofficially diagnosed A.D.D., I started counting sheep, my head spins, 101 Dalmatians, McDonald's farm full of animals, and twelve hundred partridges in both pear and apple trees.

So many times I wondered, oh brother, where art thou brains? If they weren't egging the neighbor's screens, they were placing dead insects inside my slippers. And don't get me started on farts. Like cars, brothers should be smog tested every year. I acquired a wealth of education from the pneumatic stinky instructors. I was in tenth grade when my oldest brother taught me to skip school by hanging out at his friend's house with his buddies. I played eenie meenie miney moe, wondering which of his buddies would be worthy enough to be my future boyfriend. That was the day I realized aliens really do reside on earth and can remove beer bottle caps with their teeth. I showed up to the day party with cocktail wieners while some guy showed up with rolled doobies. I knew something was strange when the teen started making sandwiches with vanilla wafers, lunchmeat, and Lucky Charms. Fortunately I wasn't introduced to the white powdery stuff razored into rows. The adventure had already broadened interactions with the principal and the police. I overheard my brother talking about having sex. Naked girly posters were a far-fetched way of achieving that goal. So were inflatable dolls. I would have gotten a lot of satisfaction out of handing one of those over to our parents.

 I preferred that my brothers went outside and tortured mice with sling shots instead of me. Certain things may have conspired to rob them of their ability to be civil. Like starting the day with excessive amounts of sugared Kool-Aid. No matter how much they cajoled their way into stirring up sympathy with Mom and Dad, nothing they said was going to stop me from turning state's evidence and having them placed permanently in some penitentiary. It would have been the perfect "Go to your room," with no release date. It was my idea to lay land mines around their beds. But for some reason, my parents weren't too keen on that proposition.

 When I was about seventeen, a younger brother told

me his co-worker wanted to take me out to dinner. I thought he'd hook me up with the cute one. It never occurred to me that the date might be a cad and predominantly lustful. What he thought was an ironclad opportunity for intimate relations, I felt was more of a Samantha moment from *Bewitched*. I would have twitched my nose, and had a guillotine dropped on his swelling phallus. It was bad enough the disgusting drive-through taco dinner landed in his lap making his groin area even more of a beefy mess. He tried kissing me and I fled like a bat outta hell. The date lasted all of fourteen minutes. It was just a tiny foretaste of what was to come with dating. Despite my rancorous resentment, I liked my brother. Love was way too strong a sentiment.

    I was a pre-teen when Mom took us to the neighbor's pool one afternoon for a swim. I was among the sun baked brood of amateur swimmers lacking in life guard training. Mumsy got a little distracted, as we all do, enjoying a cocktail. Understandably so, having thirteen children between them who were mostly boys. I was surprised she didn't say, "Mom's on martini break, swim at your own risk." Meanwhile, the rascal kinsmen of impractical jokes pulled funnies by diving in and bobbing up and down gasping for air, making my mother a wreck. I detected another problem. I spotted a small bare-chested body submerged for a spell, wondering which brother it was. The one who used my favorite shoes for smashing caterpillars? Or the one who once brought me mayo in a cup mixed with horseradish and told me it was vanilla pudding? So I wasn't too quick in rescuing the mystery boy by jumping into a cold marinating pee pond just to pull out any irritator who made my life miserable. If I had been drowning, I could easily envision my male relations stealing the pretzels off my paper plate instead of saving me. Besides, my boobs weren't exactly of Dolly Parton proportions that would aid as a proper flotation system. Even though it wasn't my job to make sure my brothers surfaced, it was probably best that mom didn't go home with one less child. Accredited with life guarding, my oldest brother acted quickly and saved the day. Twenty-five years passed, and I was partying at my parent's pool with my own toddler, when another brother dove in to save her after her unexpected immersion. With my heart sinking as well, it didn't take me long to realize my brothers aren't always boneheads. They will lay down their lives for me, and I them. But if I get pushed into a pool and drown, motives will likely be questioned.

Good Deeds

Someone once said, the smallest good deed is better than the grandest intention. Tyler Perry did a "Good Deed" by helping a single mother with much-needed stability. Bono does good deeds with his humanitarianism. Clifford teaches lighthearted lessons on the value of helping others. I resolved to do one good deed daily during this holiday season. This week I am going to save on water by drinking hot toddies, leave peppermint bark on cars in store parking lots, take pizzas to employees at burger franchises, and drop off Victoria Secret catalogs to fire stations for firefighter's entertainment during down times. A lot of people expect something in return for their good deeds. Not that I need something in return, but if my house ever catches fire, those enchanting fire extinguishers will be there in two seconds flat. And I will do everything those helpful and handsome laddermen tell me to do.

My parents instilled in me the goodness of giving which eventually carried over into my adult life. Sainthood sort of ran in our family. Dad almost became a devout Jesuit priest until he succumbed to female allurement and married my mother. Then Mom progressed with fellowship by birthing a brood in between volunteering at church. I myself sat in pews week after week nodding off during dullish homilies, and praying for a little role reversal. God could be me, and I wanted to play God. I was convicted several times for petitioning both the pastor and the pope with my wise cracking ideas. However I did try following in the path of my parents by helping out. Like the time Momma asked where her eyeglasses were. I found them upstairs and proceeded to get them to her promptly by sending them down the banister in a laundry basket. I guess I had bobsledding on my mind.

I also engaged in the kindly act of shoveling snow by compacting eight inches of blizzardy substance onto the entire entryway making it into one heck of a slippery slide. In my defense, I was three. As I got older, I helped out by washing colored towels in Clorox without being asked. There's been so much skepticism whether or not there's intelligence on other planets. I'm sure my parents wondered if there would ever be intelligence in their own household. In order to be older and wiser, I suppose we have to start out younger and dumber. Even though I never aspired to be a saint, I still felt the humongous temptation to be a good human being. Besides, if I didn't practice acts of kindness, I wouldn't get Christmas presents.

One year my own daughters and I took gifts to the hospital children's ward on Christmas Day. Another season I took my youngest to a senior assisted-living facility where we sang Christmas canticles. I can tell you this. I am far more likely to be killed by a falling coconut than by a bunch of elders who don't appreciate off-key caroling during the holiday season. It also tickled my heart helping an older lady friend rake her leaves, even though I expelled bitter expletives every time the wind picked up and blew the leaves all over the lawn again. The breezy unfairness could have kept me from ever offering to rake again.

I was smack dab in the middle of being awesome on another occasion when I helped a girlfriend carry stacks of books and other items for her yard sale. Blood saturated her two dollar lamp shade after my nasty paper cut. I endured yet another blow when she backed into her ten dollar rusty bicycle that fell into my shin, making memories that would last us both a lifetime. In the words of *Crowded House*, such love can make you weep, or make you run for cover. I did a major courtesy by not asking why she was selling her Mont Blanc pen and fourteen Chia Pets. Her plan was to get rid of everything and my plan was to not die from blood loss or tetanus in the process. Even though I sustained injuries to the tibialis and the nociceptor, I went home a hero. I expected to be in full finger and leg strength two days afterwards for my next good deed.

My boyfriend is a good-deeder. One day while leaving a restaurant with a bag of leftovers, we walked by a man who asked, "Got a hundred?" Now beggars normally ask for a dollar, or a quarter, or your whole wallet if they are holding a gun to your head. We thought it was rather gutsy of this guy and offered him our food instead. Walking away, apprehension begat kindred visions of kindness within my boyfriend's soul. "I should have given him a hundred," he said, regretting it ever since. More recently while valet parking at a hotel, the young attendant turned over our keys and my guy reluctantly announced, "I only have a hundred." The teen told us, "That's okay, don't worry about it." Superb timing coupled with my beau's huge heart prompted him to hand the kid a hundred dollar bill. You would have thought he gave the teen a Ferrari. I myself don't have that kind of currency to hand over. I'm more prepared to do a quick distracting dance routine or say, "Awww, would ya look at that! There's a family of squirrels!"

God put me on this planet to accomplish a number of things. A warm chestnut praline latte is one way to a joyful existence, especially if I buy one for the person behind me at Starbucks. I did rob a restaurant a few times, but did my good deeds by returning their pens. And I'm forever replacing toilet paper rolls since some desperate soul may be the next person to need it. Those who can't say something nice should say it in pig Latin, or Yiddish, or at least fake Chinese, then repudiate with kind words and actions because saying and doing positive things have equal powers of well being. My beau compliments me continuously by expressing, "I hope your day is as nice as your butt." It doesn't get any better than that. I return the kindful praises by telling him, "I'm glad you aren't a nut-case!" He assures me, "I'm glad you are!"

The Fugitive

How can a girl be blamed for baneful behavior when she has sat in front of the television tube absorbing the antics that shows like *Dark Shadows* and *Have Gun, Will Travel* presented? It was right around my seventeenth year of living when I subconsciously ran away. Never mind that I had every reason to take off after residing in a suburban *Twilight Zone*, where three sibling dames and six *Dukes of Hazard* were totally on top of me and my every move. Our *Family Affair* was a minefield. I would have liked more of a *Laugh-In*.

One high school chum and I thought the *Days of Our Lives* needed spontaneity and seeing what was beyond our stifling ranch style homes. It was characteristic of *Bonanza*, as if Little Joe was going to saunter in applauding our impetuous efforts to run wild and free. We were destined to play all day hooky then go see Jethro Tull in a downtown Detroit concert hall. And without so much as a mention to my makers where the teens in transit were going or that we would be gone for enough hours to put out an APB. I shoved my job aside and called in sick. Except that my curious boss unexpectedly phoned my house wondering how *The Fugitive* was feeling. I had a legitimate excuse. I woke up in a great mood and didn't want to ruin it by going to work. I told him that I had contracted a severely infectious disease that was currently wreaking havoc on my household. In closing arguments, *The Flying Nun* messed up. I reassured them that Patty Duke did some pretty intense scheming at times.

Parents fear that their daughters will get caught up in the shark-infested streets of the city. Where some girls might seek out thrills and fortune from street corner johns, this *Maverick* just wanted to hear some brilliant flute playing. *Different Strokes* for different folks I suppose. I like to say that a kid as innocent as the Beav got lured away by a female Eddie Haskell, or got *Lost in Space*. No one was going to believe the latter. Yet I had already moved on from *Petticoat Junction* to leather hot pants and platform heeled music theatres, though not yet ready for pimping myself out 77 times on a *Sunset Strip*. I was sure my parents *Ozzie & Harriet* wouldn't have wanted me coming to them impregnated and saying, "*I've Got A Secret!*"

Thank goodness my covetous caretakers didn't call the *Highway Patrol*. The next thing we knew, we were plucked off the concert steps after closing and were returned to our rightful owners. I decided to *Get Smart* and go home to my *Little House on the Prairie* with none other than my uncle, who showed up depicted as *Baretta*. Dad didn't come looking for me. It was the final night of hockey season. And Mom was too busy worrying and chugging a whole bottle of Chablis. I'm sure she was commiserating with Del Shannon, wa wa wa wa wondering why I ran away, and where I would stay.

I came home to a bunch of lined up Brady's ready to take jabs at me, right before they had my picture plastered all over milk cartons and got rid of all my stuff. With primeval gypsy articulation, I choked out the clarification that my girly friend was running away and I didn't want her going alone. It was the truth. I doubt the speakers of the house believed me because they started mimicking *Lassie* by barking orders. They sounded like government interrogators with their systematic torture, ready to detain me for the rest of my tormented teen life. If we had lived on a *Love Boat*, I wouldn't have had this much difficulty adapting to squalls. Although with my girlfriend fleeing her more turbulent household, I figured she didn't have near as many *Happy Days* as I did.

My parents could have survived an earth shattering Scud missile, but not have their precious perfect Catholic daughter tainted by improper escapades. They would have preferred that I stayed chained in the dungeon... had our home been blessed with a basement. But I did have restricted air space within the confines of my bedroom with three sisters, and six *Bewitched* brothers whom every hour would open and slam my bedroom door and sometimes throw in a reptile, leaving me to be tortured by a blunt snouted scaly aggressor with freakish skin warts. I'd *Dream of a Genie* with high hopes that my every rub of the lantern would eliminate it, and my brothers. It was a painful transition from being worldly to becoming an imprisoned criminal. There was something very Alfred Hitchcock-y about it because throughout my formative years, I was told that there wasn't a monster in the closet or under the bed.

My parents taught me *The Facts of Life*. But my pouty lips were prone towards kissing, largely due to the productions of *Dallas* and *Knots Landing*. I could have done worse than swapping saliva and running off for a day. Lucky for them I was just an *American Bandstand*er, rock and rolling nights away on dance floors. My parents should have been grateful that I didn't turn into little miss sure shot like *Annie Oakley*. Who knows if they considered disowning me, wanting to send me off in a *Taxi* to go live with pedigree that might mirror *The Munsters* or *The Addams Family*, where I would have parents like Morticia and Gomez and an Uncle Fester providing me with maniacal life lessons. I would have been very leery of having another Pugsly type brother who pulled villainous pranks.

Once released from the bedroom shackles, I never cruised *The Outer Limits* again. However, I will be going to hell for making my parents sweat for fifteen hours. I'm thankful that my uncle didn't come after me in a moving vehicle, making me a casualty of domestic war. Although ending up in a surgical care *M*A*S*H* unit under the watchful eyes of Hawkeye Pierce and Trapper John would have been *Good Times*. They would have had mascara running down my face in a matter of minutes. I would rather have died from injury and laughing than be killed by my parents.

Adding to the list of many juvenile influences, Lucy and Red Skelton have most certainly left lasting side effects as well. We are what we watch.

Lordess of the Rings

There is usually not a time when I can't take a phone call—barring bath time, mealtime, or just plain social anxiety. My oldest daughter left a message yesterday to call her back. Concerned if it was something important, I called back right away. I left a long message relaying crucial information that my age spots are now multiplying and my belly has gone beyond its alluring limit. I know how exciting my precious phone call must have meant to her because when I called again she didn't answer. Once I did get a hold of her she pleaded, "Gotta call you back. I might be able to make a baby, the postman is here." This sort of zany exchange is true confirmation of our wacky kinship. Something must have come up, because I waited a full fifty-three seconds, and she still hadn't called back.

This same daughter abides by the aphorism "Live long and pester." It brings back memories of my childhood days with our retro rotary wall phone and its unlimited amount of annoyers. I mean users. More often than not, my nine siblings and I all scurried at the same time with the boisterous longing to hear who was on the other end. What can I say other than we had poor impulse control. I was often terrorized by the maze of traffic that whizzed by me aimed at answering the thing. I was knocked to the ground on several occasions and wanted to die peacefully like my mother did in later years. Not be fatally crushed by the many children she bore. I did have to commend my adoring siblings on the prompt and timely manner in which they trampled people. If only they had been that quick when asked to do the dishes.

I implicated certain siblings in the run-by-shootings procured by water pistols when I was spending too much time on the phone myself. They pointed weapons of tree branches, poking me throughout my whole conversations. I was taught that using scream tactics should at all times be avoided. I needed to wait till I got off the phone before yelling back at them and deafening the person on the other end. I thought to myself, what would Jesus want me to do? I was 95% sure He wouldn't want me strangling my siblings with the phone cord. Whoever said "give me a home where the buffalo roam" had never lived on our range. For someone who commingled with a stampede of wild boars and would someday need to be reprogrammed into polite society, it's no wonder I still snort when I laugh.

The telephone at times was crucially needed, and at other times was a trap for useless information. I never wanted to be greeted with the pressure of mortality at ten years old when a funeral home called asking if we had already purchased our plots. Fifteen was an even tougher year when I ran for the Bell system with every reverberation, hoping the school football team had my number. We racked up a lot of miles wearing down kitchen linoleum. As if it was a caller fictitiously awarding our family with an-all-expense-paid-trip to Fiji. We were fortunate if we got to the end of our street.

Mom ended up cutting me off cold-phone-turkey after I accepted a collect call from Monaco. I thought it was her friend Monica. And our neighbor called continuously wanting to borrow things. We had already loaned him half a bag of fertilizer, the grill, and fifty bucks. Little did I know that nothing had been returned, and he wanted to borrow our new lawn mower. Obligingly, I took it right over. Another day the gynecologist's office called, and I relayed the message to mom that her Pabst beer was inconsistent. Maybe I heard things wrong, but I thought mom was a regular wine drinker. Yet it was another sibling prankster who should have gotten in far more trouble for answering the phone imparting, "Roses are red, boogers are green, I'll only respond, if you say something obscene."

    One time during my teenage, phone hogging, one brother quipped, "Your call is extremely important to me. Please enjoy this endless drum solo while I wait," as he beat away at the walls around me. I tried to redirect his attention by telling him that Bigfoot was in the back yard but somehow he didn't believe me. I realized that pleasing him was impossible, but making his blood boil was easy. Although not all counsel is created equal. Mom said to hang up and ponder the virtues of silence. Dad said to stop monopolizing the receiver and stretching the coiled cord into my room, or he'd rip the ringer from the wall. This might have been a strong indication that I was a stinker. Not so, when someone else pulled the phone into the pantry while trying to spread peanut butter on Saltines, thus entwining peanutty stickiness into the coiling line. The exfoliation however certainly increased the cord skins capacity to be more flexible and reduce any wrinkles.

    As one Lordess of Rings to another, I wanted to help my mother with what I thought was the perfect solution to phone grabbing. I told her to spike my sibling's milk with barbiturates. Mom couldn't bring herself to do it, but she could have diverted the phone seizers by keeping bottles of bubbles nearby as deterrents, specifically for those restless beings whose phone waiting impatience was so bothersome. She should have also had several coin operated telephone booths installed in different areas of the house. The financial intake coming from those phones could have assured her that trip to Fiji.

Times have changed. The last thing I want to be doing is spending countless hours on the telephone. No one will want to talk to me anyway if I'm fueled by a cocktail or three. Where was the happy when I balanced holding the phone while I was slaving over a hot stove at the same time the cat was playing tackle with my ankles? I prefer that people send me a message in a bottle that has been tossed into the middle of the Pacific.

Against One's Will

My mother once told me I was destined for drama on the big screen. She also told me I was destined to be handcuffed to my bedroom drawer handle never to go out of the house again if I didn't clean my room. And beating a wooden spoon against my headboard to get me out of bed in the morning didn't make me move any faster. My life would have been so much better had I added and enforced a nonrestrictive clause to her commands. I'm sure Mom would have cried if I ran away, although she probably cried when I didn't. I just hope all the protests I demonstrated didn't spoil her enjoyment of parenting.

Another thing my creators did against my will was wash my hair in the tub when I was a toddler. Water always got into my eyes. Then Mama added a few sisters, which made way too many Tinkel-belles in the bathwater. Pee in the wash basin is probably the main reason I have all these side effects. That kind of urethra release does not boost the stimulation of any swimmer or bather. I didn't need the exothermic expulsion of other sibling's body fluids. I loved my family, but not when the bathtub was turned into a blemished body of liquid set for stewing in someone's juices. Mom told me to stay in the contaminated reservoir until I was clean, which made no sense to me. Nowadays I take long soothing bubble baths without anyone whom I think might taint my tub.

Playing has long been a pre-occupation with me, such as dressing the dog in a bonnet and forcing him into a baby buggy when I was eight. I couldn't figure out why he didn't want to be held captive while being whipped around the driveway at warp speeds. He was a little scared of me. Once I found our pooch four blocks away, I held him down again attempting to comb his hair. I also liked playing school in the garage but my siblings didn't like being forced against their will to sit there as students. It was the main reason they started skipping class. That, and the fact that I made them sit up straight and give me a list of conjunctive adverbs. I didn't know any, so someone had to tell me what they were. I never paid any attention to my teachers either. Detainees just can't stand the emotions that we are called upon to endure. Lunchtime was the only thing that induced any kind of pleasure, although I would have enjoyed my life ten times more if I had been eating at the state beach instead of an educational facility. I asked Mom on several occasions if I could play hooky. But she said hell had already frozen over and was not accepting any more demonstrative adolescents.

One time our cat caught a cricket and would not let go without a fight. It was a clear indication of who wanted custody. That bit of weevil and feline tenacity taught me never to be held hostage against my free will. They'd have to threaten me with a branding iron first. Now that I think about it, bureaucratic tax enforcement agents hold me hostage. I will eventually pay what I owe, even if I have to borrow from the federal government to do it. After postmortem pet lizard, came my mother's investigation into the postmortem piggy bank. I filled coins faithfully into my pink hog after my parent's insistence on saving. Coming from a large family, we never asked for anything when Mom and Dad went to a store. So I just assumed that my savings was the only way to get red licorice. I retreated to my bedroom on one occasion searching for the omnivorous container holding the coins that would cover the cost of my craving. Then I ran for the hammer, obviously prepared to bust the bank. Evidently it's bad form using this sort of tool with overt aggressiveness thus having shrapnel and shards of ceramic flying and poking holes in a lamp shade. It ended in mortal conflict with my Mama. Not to mention siblings hovering with stares and appreciative scowls like I was robbing a Brinks truck or something. If my mother had known I was saving for a Mark Eden breast developer, maybe she would have let me spend my money on licorice. Being thoroughly interrogated, I became troubled with her line of questioning and was forced to stay home. I felt it was a bit hasty, never mind totally against my will to be that claustrophobically confined to my sleeping quarters. I wanted to move to Peru where goats could raise me. Though I doubt goats are that great to live with either.

No one wants to be held coercively, especially by nail cosmeticians. The last one I visited planted me in a spa chair and submerged my feet in a rushing vat of scalding water made of certain crystals and, for all I know, the glands and guts of a desert mole rat. Then she disappeared for the next forty-five excruciating minutes. I continued my spasmodic attacks of pure toenail neglect, brought on by this foreign speaking woman who totally held me at her mercy. She strolled by me several times saying, "I be there two minute." I started a series of interesting sounds, none remotely pleasant or admired by fellow spa sitters. I would have left had my hooves not transformed into trench feet, plus my nails still needed pruning and polishing. Too much water is just a recipe for dermatitis. Maybe she didn't know my day was filled with other vital activities like the supermarket triathlon and cleaning the cupboard calisthenics. My salonist originally assured me of a prompt time frame, but cheated me out of valuable post office step aerobics as well. I should have been handed a free coupon for my next visit: "Good for One Rapturous Day in Spa Prison." Those spa people sure look at you funny when you leave chewed gum on the armrest as a tip.

Love is a Many Censored Thing

My brain was my most superlative organ, up until I fell in love the first time. I was thirteen. Not a single force on earth could stop my trembling body. I had to suffer through the entire school year before seeing this guy at my grandparent's cottage every summer. He and his cousins occupied two cabins across the lake. You sure learn to swim in a hurry when there's a cute bushy blonde on the other side you want to manhandle. I was either going to swim across for some great kisses, or I was going to die trying. I made that decision in thirty feet of lake water and have survived to tell about it.

Recently I ran across a stack of love letters from my first crush. I probably should have sued him for fraud after he told me he would love me forever and went on to marry another woman. Love seemed so eternal at the time. One year my siblings and I contracted mumps and the measles and I sat lakeside staring at his cabin. I could only see him from a distance, and it was pure agony. The next year we were like animals in heat. I had practically planned our futures together, although our unworldly and callow innocence kept us from even touching each other. That Christmas, I was hoping that my true love would send me that golden ring. When I didn't get one in the mail, my heart continued to beat despite the imaginary knife that was wedged inside it. Even though I would have liked a sleepover with this friend every single night of the week, I wasn't exactly ready to be tied down to holy wedlock at fourteen. There are many men who make one common mistake when they get married. They stop flirting with their wives. In all fairness, women make chocolate a priority over men every day.

The year after that I was a little older, but not that much wiser when I was willing to pick out plate patterns after playing spin-the-bottle in his barn. As if a kiss solidified our relationship. There were about eight of us twirling the empty glass decanter along with my boyfriend's wily wise guy of a cousin, who also had a hopeless crush on me. He thought it was love at first sight. I still didn't think it was love at tenth sight. I suspected that he came from The Garden of Eden where strutting around in a bulging loincloth was fashionable. I was hesitant in playing the bottle game since he tried directing the thing straight at me every time we played. I refused to kiss him because after that, he would have wanted to play naked Twister. I had a very hard time liking the brown eyed boy who kept saying, "Just digest those butterflies, baby." At the time, I thought he was a scoundrel. Yet it was possible that he was just missing some nutrient-rich foods in his diet that would make him more pleasing to my eyes and ears. Such as choline, for normal brain development. I wasn't sure. All I knew was that my tingles were reserved for his captivating cousin.

But the stalker wouldn't go away. I would get up in the morning and stroll outside where he would be hiding around every corner. He caught me very serenely walking through the woods and came up behind me remarking, "You seem so unhappy. I'm here to change that." A babe in timberland is susceptible to wolves and restless boys on the make. Despite all my unembellished appeals for solitude, he couldn't help himself on another occasion when we got ice cream together. He commented, "It must be love if your ice cream melted." I would have preferred that my boyfriend treated me like some majestic endangered species. Not this guy. I wanted so badly to tell my shrewd pursuant, "Meet me back in these deep dark woods at midnight." I would have shown up fully costumed in Reaper gear, ready for a castration.

After summer vacations, I went home and looked every day for the mailman to come, waiting for those love letters from my crush. One day I opened a note that read, "I miss you. Probably not near as much as you miss me, but I'm an awesome catch." It was from the boy I despised. Every summer I would see him again and he gave me several more good reasons not to date him. He could make me cringe. He could pump blood faster than he could pump gas. His idea of multi-tasking was talking to several girls at once. Only I had to dismiss that reason since he asked a few gals in the store where the floral department was so he could buy me roses. Yet it was another unfavorable omen when my fingers touched their thorns. I wanted a love like Richard and Liz, Brad and Angie, Morticia and Gomez, Romeo and Juliet. But I also wanted a relationship that would last longer than five days, and I surely wouldn't commit to mutual suicide.

Many years later, I was curious to know if I would be attracted to that loathsome lad at the cottage and choose him instead over my crush. Doting can go a long way. Maybe I should have accepted his fourteen marriage proposals. I went on to marry as well, but found matrimony to be very complex and psychological. One mate ends up becoming a bit psycho, and the other more logical. In my case, don't ask me who was who.

Barbies vs. Kens

Ah, relationships. That enigmatic chore of gaining leverage with the opposite sex. I have enough stories from my past till the cows come home. Unlike horses, who usually return to their stables rather quickly.

All I ever needed to know about love I thought came from having both Barbie and Ken dolls. Time I could have spent learning a few other ways, like taking binoculars to drive-in theatres. Or hanging out in my parent's closet pretending to sort suits and dresses, hoping I would catch mummy and daddy in action. Although, if I had caught them doing anything, I would have felt more at home wearing a rooster costume to a cockfight.

I could have become jailbird Barbie after slaughtering the boys who ruthlessly feasted their eyes on my body parts. Because back then, Mother Nature lined me up healthily and anatomically correct. Yet unlike most Barbies, I had a gross deficiency in the glamorous life and accessories. I'm not sure why my parents went to all the expense of fixing my crooked teeth to look like Mattel's beautiful creation, only with a tad larger midsection and not so perfect ribcage. It wasn't until later that I thought about also living my life in plastic.

When I reached the age of almost married, I was told by Dr. Ruth to greet my guy at the door wearing nothing but Cool Whip. Which meant I could use my anatomically correct chassis to delude a dude if I wanted to. You know, that one aspect of matrimonial training that had yet to be implemented. Unfortunately I wasn't making a Kraft dessert at the time, so I was out of the creamy topping. I opted for salsa. And since it was hockey season, I spelled out GOAL with tortilla chips across my bedding. Unfortunately my boytoy's lunging technique failed, and he tripped over my entry mat slamming his head into the door jamb causing instantaneous trauma to his motor region. He never even paused long enough to notice my frontal buttons covered in his favorite snack. I held back my surging passion to rush him to Emergency, grabbing whatever I could to cover me, which would easily have been a pickle fork and a salad spinner. Except it was cold outside. But I must say, I was hot, as in habenero. I would have married crippled Ken despite his yelling at me for having a dangerous door mat, and the intermittent paralysis on his face. And, if he wasn't so hell bent on bringing his buddies on the honeymoon.

All men need the sensitivity to swerve away from pedestrians, and not turn the streets into speedways. One raggedy Andy came over one day to help me wash my car and nearly took out the whole neighborhood. I wanted him to come inside to trap a cockroach. Later I found a strange toothbrush in my bathroom, his slippers under my bed, and the roaming roach still surveying his breeding ground. Moving in together can be adventurous, provided you like the person, and that he's skillfully accomplished in cornering common house invaders. Romeo and Juliet's love story didn't end well either. I have this thing for sharpened knives and drinking yucky stuff that might force me into a permanent sleep. Although I was out to find someone who would totally kill himself for me.

In the event that an action packed G. I. Joe appeared to devote his time to marital bliss, there were other requirements. Such as planning for a family, when gamblers anonymous Ken wanted to invest in every slot machine in Vegas. It would have been totally fine if he was prepared to live with catatonic Barbie. And sluggish Ken sat on the couch way too often. I was probably on NyQuil when I accepted that marriage proposal. Or maybe I just wanted a few fondue sets and a gravy boat. If it was any hormonal indication that I might be wrong on occasion, marriage sometimes isn't forever. Supposing couples never fought, they could end up with a few hundred children. Then there wouldn't be time for tiffs. I married, and divorced. Although it did end amicably. He's still alive.

Some spendthrift Kens can't splurge on dream houses. But hopefully they can afford dinners out, something more elaborate than meals wrapped in paper where Barbie can have a Frangelico with her fries. I kiss better after lobster and three goblets of fine wine. I have finally found that man, and we have just moved in together. My prince calls me his true love, so I feel more like Cinderella than Barbie. I too can get all gussied up, dance the night away, and by the end of the evening lose a shoe. And with my prince's failing eyesight, I just hope he doesn't go around town trying to find the woman who fits that shoe. I also hope he doesn't expect me to work too laboriously or sleep in the attic.

My doll and I have decided not to get married. But I would love to see Mattel manufacturing the married forever bifocals Barbie and BenGay Ken. It might put my faith back into wedded bliss. Besides, I already have a gravy boat, deviled egg carrier, nice asparagus prongs, and all the crystal I need.

Parent Trap

It began when one of my daughters remarked, "I have a brilliant beyond brilliant idea! Let's go to Universal Studios." Once again, I had fallen into the parental tourist trappings of another theme park adventure. Participants included two scheming daughters, two precocious granddaughters, and one not-so-happy-to-oblige sluggish woman (moi) who is always trying to avoid exhausting funfairs. The kids called it their fun place. I called it a magical arena full of more toys than I could afford for nine hours while pretending I could still think straight.

The granddaughters were dressed and ready to run through the fairyland. The daughters and their mother needed to be catapulted to the park, and were then espresso energized by way of Starbucks. I needed enough caffeine and carmelized sweetener to walk that communal event. I was one of those sluggish people who appreciated coffee's invigorating significance, which probably explained my electricity while dancing with my ten-month-old granddaughter, asking nothing in return but frequent pee breaks. Eight cups of water per day and I'm a casual bathroom visitor. Yet one cup of coffee and there are abnormal changes in the urinary system and the need to pee is intensified by a million. I turned into a speed demon, wanting to use the mommy-had-an-accident excuse to forge forward in bathroom lines.

We proceeded to the world of Harry Potter where we entered the main amusement ride that holds a high level of screaming activity. What looked like the cloaked headmaster of Hogwarts approached us, and my twelve-year-old granddaughter became breathlessly besotted. For a minute there, I thought Hallie Parker was my grandchild when she proclaimed, "I've dreamt of meeting you my whole life and I just hope that one day you can love me as me, and not as the person my mother thinks I am." She isn't the same freckled-faced drama queen as she is a comedic charmer. The caped wonder provided us with information about baby swap, whereas we were able to use a password to skip ahead in line and take turns on the ride. We passed people who were fixated on us with such sisterly betrayal as if we were no doubt, the lowest most awful creatures on the planet. Regardless, we still had to wait in line amongst murderous stares and with my urgency to release a stream from the front faucet yet again, if you know what I mean. And I thought a constantly weeing baby was bad. Either way, large amounts of incontinence is hard to ignore.

With my kids right behind me, I told the ride operator, "It's me or them. Take your pick." He took my kids first, probably because he didn't want to deal with projectile vomiting from a panicked elderly person who ends up freaking out on this drop tower of perpetual terror. Little did he know I needed to get on and off that thing rather quickly before it was necessary for my bladder to lower its water level again. I swear my kids were so happy to go ahead that they turned into a couple of Elvis impersonators when they told the guy, "Thankyou, thankyou ver much." I'm sure both my daughters would have liked to disclose, "She's never had one cup of triple espresso her entire life, and she shows up today totally stimulated." I could have added some spice to their non-verbal commentary by adding, "It was a little too robusk for a cup of coffee if you ask me, but then again I'm impartial to being supersonic."

Once my speedy body was on the rapid rotating track, I felt my organs floating inside me, not to mention my damp drawers. Any respectful carnival goer would have visited the restroom first so not to lubricate the seats of amusement rides. Flying high above Hogwarts castle, my eyeballs were practically forced into the back of my head. I called out to the person who was handling the contraption at the far end of the wild ride, but he couldn't hear me above my gasping or the ten million other shrieking occupants. Thankfully no kids could hear my swearing. The young male attendee watched me exit in such a way that he most surely expected me to go weak in the knees and fall into his arms and sob hysterically. Okay, I did cry hard, and tears fell down my legs. My trembling frame staggered off looking pale as school chalk with vessels bulging in my forehead, and with wet panties. Holding it in was just as hard as trying to control the bamboo in my yard. I'm sure the other riders thought I was the bloody incontinent ghost of Christmas past. Nothing would have pleased me more than to say, "Being older and incontinent is not a crime you know."

I wasn't prepared for another landing. Once three o'clock rolled around, I was jolted away from the coffee's potency and very close to collapsing. I ended up flat on my back in line at the Simpson's motion simulator ride where it was open season for the frenzied whir of passersby. It was time to go home to a glass of something that would relax me. When I did, I told my girls, "Here's to you. May your lives be far less complicated than mine."

Let me sum up this theme park adventure. I had a great time. I now have a new loan to pay. Next time I'll be wearing something for the weak end, or make my bladder gladder by not going at all. And I'm writing this from my bed because I still haven't recovered.

Guess: Writer's block? Spider phobia? Doing something fun with insomnia? Or just plain pooped and too tired to participate?

Artsy Fartsy

I have done a lot of artwork in my day. It started very young, although I don't recall my drawings ever being displayed on the refrigerator. I thought they were good. But I suppose they weren't refrigerator good. Some of them must have been garbage good when I found a few in the trash. Of course I did have a rather active imagination. But If I had been a horrid artist and an even horrider child, I would have been drawing skulls and crossbones on doors instead of flowers and people on paper. I asked my mother about my many missing popsicle stick and elbow pasta project pieces. She squirmed delinquently. I'm sure it was very itchy and painful to have to fess up to the fact that she fed the landfill with my fine works of craftsmanship.

Mom must have asked me a million times to brush my teeth. Eventually she told me that I didn't have to brush all of them, just the ones I wanted to keep. This is how artistic I really was. She found me in the bathroom brushing but declared snidely, "Nice use of watercolors, but you were assigned to brush with toothpaste." I could have really made her mad by brushing my teeth with glitter glue or food coloring. I should mention the time I was sentenced to four hours of cabinetry crayoned removal service. That night at dinner, she mentioned the benefits of joining art classes in Singapore. She couldn't lose me to another country, not when I became the teen who decorated all the place cards for her dinner parties. I wanted to calligraphy hangover cures, but basic etiquette told me not to. As did my mother. I thought I was being very creative and helpful the times the doorbell rang when nobody was there, and I drew a pretty sign and sat it outside our front entrance that read: "Doorbell ringers and runners will be executed to the fullest extent by the dog, and the boys who reside here."

Think about this. My mother had ten children. Multiply that by crayons, paints, pastels, glue, and palettes of paper. Being left alone to create something with all these things is a pretty strong indication that a gaggle of kids are going to draw, tint, or use Stickum on something they aren't suppose to. It was just my rotten luck that sibling six leaned on a paint tube sending the splattering colorant all over sibling four. And sibling five cut and glued the tablecloth. We were blissfully unaware that my mother was hovering nervously from the doorway. Nobody knows the trouble I've seen. Just because I was oldest in the birth order and so depended upon, she shot a look at me like she might be contemplating homicide. Funny, but after that she still continued to bring more children into the world. She's lucky that my baby brother's sagging diaper contents that smelled like the Denver Arapahoe Disposal Site didn't end up being hand painted all over her furniture. But there were several crepe paper rolling Rembrandts running through the house. As a result, Mom ended up being quite skillful in several languages. English, sarcasm, mockery, and profanity. Usually with the eldest, there's a spectacular scrapbook saved with many original memories. The youngest is lucky if there's even a hand or footprint from birth. In my case, I don't have anything to show for my work, when my youngest sibling has enough to practically fill a museum.

Creativeness also came with stumbling blocks. In one grade school class, we were supposed to draw a feathered dinosaur. I became mystified when the head needed to emphasize reptilian scales. Then I drew feathery arm flaps but became mentally challenged with the dinosaur's beak. More importantly, how was I going to visually convey the variation from warm-blooded to cold-blooded? The worst part was when someone ran off with my pencil sharpener.

I was painting my nails artistically long before salons made it fashionable, which was a very calming and prolific way of expressing myself. Mom would tell me, "Gee, I see you're awfully good-natured today. What medium do I owe that pleasantness to?" I told her that she should be colorfully artistic herself by having all of our names tattooed on her body. But she said that she already had a multitude of tattoos in the form of stretchmarks.

The day came when I told my parents that I really needed to focus on my art. They wanted to send me to Pratt Institute, one of the leading colleges of art and design. Yet they couldn't afford to feed me much less send me to a prominent school in Manhattan. I sometimes wonder whether it was me, or if I heard my mother snickering while saying that she'd rather jet me off to boarding school. Who knows if Pratt would have turned me away saying, "We really love your work, but..." Heavily encumbered with my mental collegiate defeat, I was staring down the path of burger flipping, wondering how I would handle the pressure of people who needed something from me when they asked, "Can I have two large fries please?" Instead, I have become extremely well educated in perseverance, child rearing, and figs. I found out there are quite a number of things you can do with figs. I've eaten them, and used them fig-uratively when it came to writing my pieces. Better to know extensively about aggregate fruit than become possibly a crack whore.

When I lived in Michigan, there was a period when I made chairs out of cut wood and washed up branches from the shores of Lake Erie. I must have built fifty of them. But there were emotional stages of furniture assembly, and it was always when I was in the worst mental states that I cranked out my best artwork. Sometimes I turned a thicket of trees into goddamn sawdust. To think I could have been a carpenter. I never produced anything that Michelangelo or Leonardo Da Vinci might look at. But being creative now keeps me from sitting around aimlessly or taking on other more disreputable hobbies. Like prank calling people I don't know, or choking on big cigars.

Starstruck

There's one precious thing I gave my mother besides three glorious granddaughters. A little piece of Paul Newman.

It was Grand Prix weekend in Detroit twenty some odd years ago, and my mother was visiting me for a few days. I had just moved into a townhouse, so she delighted and amazed this house host with unpacking, room organization, and deep cleaning from ceiling to floor grout. And when I say cleaning, I mean disinfection and deodorizing as if she was sanitizing surgical equipment in an operating room. If we were eating meals and I got up to go to the bathroom, I was surprised she didn't clean and wax my wood chair while I was gone. I was already high on life. Double high once mom left vapors of ammonia. Needless to say, she was pooped after all her laborious workouts. Too pooped to go out with me and enjoy her several sips of Chablis in our annual happy hour excursions.

One night I had plans to meet up with several friends at a local Italian eatery and my mother stayed behind. We knew the waiter who approached informing us that race car driver Paul Newman was dining behind drapery in a separate room. There were stocky, grizzly bear type bodyguards securing the area, ready to claw anyone that came past the barricade to interrupt Paul's meal with any of their stalking maneuvers. It was like trying to look behind the Iron Curtain. It pained me that my mother was sitting at home instead of with me where she could be pining for her idol in person. She could have possibly been the person in charge of feeding the dashing and debonair man grapes, or fanning him and diverting those Michigan mosquitos that hot summer night.

    The eatery was both a restaurant and a bar, so my friends and I proceeded to get a drink at the bar and snack on spinach dip while waiting for the Grand Prix honoree to leave. I had schemed a thorough exit scenario in my head, mostly because my mother would totally want me to touch the guy so I could go home and touch her. I called it association by handshake or suffocating bear hug. My big plan was to bolt out the bar entrance door and meet him on the sidewalk, hoping that I didn't have spinach sprouting from my teeth. I must remember never to eat greens right before approaching a major movie star. I don't normally go around skulking into other people's lives unless there's a darn good reason to skulk. Except ambushing is usually when two people are meeting on a sidewalk together, and only one of them knows about it. Perhaps he would just see me as an unpaid bodyguard, not a star thirsty psychobabe. My harmless observation did make me wonder if he ever got the feeling that he was being watched. I wanted to explain to him that it wasn't my car sitting in his driveway on those many occasions. I've never done anything crazy, except for the time I was a youngster on my bicycle throwing Bit-O-Honeys to pedestrians and telling them bees were sure to follow.

    What I had was a cool hand Luke moment, and a failure to communicate. I didn't want to stand on the sidewalk and stare. I read that when a person stares, their pupils dilate 45% larger. And it isn't necessarily a result from wearing contact lenses inside out. I entertained thoughts of craziness again by getting down on all fours and conjuring up some baseless narrative that I was discovering a cure for cracked cement. Or explain why certain ants survive pedway living. Either way, crouching down could have created some serious problems. The last thing I wanted was for him to not see me, trip and fall, kill himself, and leave his wife to hunt me down with revenge. It was dark, so I could have shammed him into thinking I was Harry Reasoner wanting an interview. I could have also belted out, "My mom has a killer crush on you," and hopefully say it without all the charm of Lizzie Borden. I began thinking that bringing up clutches and carburetors might be good topics since the man was car crazy. Although I might have been better off singing the classic Dean Martin tune "How Lucky Can One Girl Be" in four part harmony. But my singing skills would only get me close to a vocal coach. I tend to talk to myself when needing expert advice on what to do in situations like this. I kept busy perfecting my introduction techniques. Unlike Paul, who perfected everything including acting, coffee, and savoir-fare.

The moment finally arrived, and the mighty Mr. Newman came out smiling at me, opening that huge door to smile back and say something constructive. What I saw was a man who remained ageless and who made facial lines look fabulous. I was hoping he'd say the same about me. I didn't know what else to do other than express my heartfelt feelings, reach for his hand then blurt out, "Darn, Joanne found you first." He chuckled, and I slipped away. He probably never believed that I was just doing this for my mother.

Life only stops at train tracks, and when you have just touched Paul Newman. Worry wormed its horrid way back in when I realized I may have soiled his palm with chip and dip remains. He had no idea the verbal stuff I held back. Feeling complete, I stepped away from him as giddy as a lynx that had found its prey. I couldn't wait to get home and shake my mother's hand to give her that little piece of Paul Newman. I told her that lots of liquor gave me the guts to approach him. She was surprised that I wasn't arrested for spunk and unsoberly.

Crimes and Missed-Demeanor

There's a comedian in every classroom. I suppose that's where my boyfriend began his crafty and celebrated skill as a comic, making his mark as the class clown throughout high school. I only wish I'd been a fly on the walls to hear all the rascality, and done some crazier things myself. Born a worrier and not a warrior, I was far too afraid of being shoved off to boarding school for misconduct, or entrusted to the care of strict disciplinarians in some foreign nunnery. So I chortle abundantly at my suitors non-regrettable stories.

We recently gathered with friends and their significant others who told stories about high school some fifty years ago. They say what you are comes from who you hang around with. I didn't know I was hanging around such delinquent legends whose ignoble acts were geared to fascinate the festal audience. The men divulged their past crimes and misdemeanors, like cherry bombing mailboxes and plate glass windows. We women had a hard time wrapping our heads around these testosterone induced conquests. One wife chimed in, "We didn't do anything like that! The girls were interested in more important things, like boys. We stood around school saying, 'That guy just looked at me! I wonder what he's thinking?' The boys stood around saying, 'Let's blow up the lockers next!'"

I was just saying how I didn't have any pyromaniac friends. I was among other ladies whose single interests in school were eyeing bad boys who didn't bother to return the attention, which left very little to our fertile female imaginations. Then we went off to play with normal people. Or cry. I can't recall. High school is really a place where the innocent and aspiring go to sow wild oats. I was writhingly unaware that I've been associating with a bunch of young and relentless hoodlums with police records. Of course my man had to relay his erstwhile antics as well. He was only listed on the school's most wanted list an indeterminable number of times. He talked about the infructuous activities such as hanging a styrofoam constructed and very erect phallic symbol from the ceiling directly over his classmates, not to mention his oblivious teacher.

    My loverboy should have gotten an observance award for the most watched composition. It had a penile circumference that would have made King Kong puny by comparison. The crime was pardoned, only by other giggling cohorts who were squirming with excitement and at the same time wondering what primate offered up this rather monumental amputation. My beau was removed from the port of sin by punishing school officials. It was right around the time that the US Civil Rights Act was passed ending discrimination in public places. It was also the same time Andy Warhol was exhibiting his pop art imagery of Campbell's soup cans. Everyone was remarking, "We'll never look at soup cans the same way again." I'm sure there was growing consensus about my boyfriend's crafty artwork that lured people into paraphrasing that statement. Anyone who went to high school will understand that hanging this type of trajectory from the classroom ceiling does cut a decent amount of geometry time. With all the capers I witnessed, no wonder I never learned Cartesian coordinates, or anything else for that matter. His caper probably concluded with a vigilant prophylactic inspection.

There's nothing like a three-week teacher sabbatical to bring out more beastly acts in my boyfriend and his buddies. Their speech teacher went out on leave and was replaced with an elderly substitute woman. The hellions immediately switched seats so they could sit together. On the instructor's first day, she asked the students to write an outline. My funny guy filled the page with Japanese symbols, and the teacher noticed the paper asking, "Mmmmm. What is this?" His buddy replied, "My friend here is a foreign exchange student from Japan, and I'm his interpreter!" Both boys began babbling in what sounded like a nonsensical East Asian dialect. The all American look of my boyfriend never even phased the gullible woman because she answered, "Oh, how wonderful! Tell him welcome to our country!" It prompted stereophonic shrills of laughter from classmates which still didn't sway the teacher. The silliness went on for three days before the long suffering principal got wind of it and pegged the boyish blunders. He said, "That wouldn't be Walton and Gonzales would it???"

There were boys in my high school who lapsed into temporary crime comas, where they too thoughtlessly cultivated ruthless paranoia throughout the legal system. Every day I'd go home and my mother would ask me, "What did you learn in school today?" I'd have to tell her that the principal passed out about ten more detention slips and the plotting dyspeptic donkeys were sequestered in the torture chamber. Breakfast clubbers know exactly what I'm talking about. There was always the detention cancellation switch when some stooge wanted to hit the emergency alarm button. Such actions sometimes resulted in suspension, which was hard on us gals when we didn't have those cute rebels around to gawk at. Once there was a rumor circling that the next afternoon's prank would involve rats. I called in sick the following day.

School staffers gave another collective groan the day Bobby, aka Bugsy Segal, one of the most infamous and feared gangsters of his day, decided to spoof one of the girls in our science class on her birthday by doing the old exploding cake trick. Imagine a fictitious cake assembled with a blown up balloon, Cool Whip for frosting, and dotted with candles doused with chemicals that can cause a nuclear reaction—ready to blow into the victims face. Though I didn't watch Mister Charismatic set it up, I did watch it mess up fellow student Laurie's flawlessly applied Maybelline. Another trickster gave her a Coke, which was really more of a soy sauce surprise in a can. This particular student was always tardy to class since she was the victim on several occasions of mind games and other misdemeanors that required her to go home to dry her eyes and change her clothes. Hers were never considered happy birthdays. I told her that hopefully the government will start deporting all the mentally ill.

My association with clowns hasn't changed much. With seniority comes a lot of silly shenanigans as well. I may be older, but I'm trying to stay young, resourceful, playful, and relentless myself. I've tried calling that clown Betty White three times this month to see if we can hang out together. I suppose I could go barricade the Starbucks bathroom door with their lounge chairs, put petroleum jelly on the escalator handrails at Nordstrom, or let crickets loose inside Costco. The supposedly sophisticated woman that I am is likely to act a little more mildly, like imitating today's twenty-year-olds by following bare legged girls around while singing, "We wear short shorts." It would never occur to them that it used to be a Nair commercial.

My maturity level ultimately depends on whom I'm with.

Out of the Mouths of Bigger Babes

I consider myself a babe sometimes, especially since I'm an older gal who still has guys looking at me. If they are gawking, it's more likely I am carrying around a trail of toilet paper that is stuck to my panties. Then I find myself acrimoniously muttering four-letter words and in the next breath, coming back to civility by saying, "Your patience during my time of venting frustration is thoroughly appreciated." Never mind the more colorful stuff that comes pouring out of my mouth when I'm pulling out said soft thin toitee layers while twenty other people are staring. Sometimes I just don't think before I speak. I do the same exact thing when I'm being passed on the freeway by some overzealous Nascar drivers. Or when I have spilled oily foods on my freshly laundered clothes. My swear jar could probably finance the entire Department of Molecular Medicine. I realize it's unladylike to curse. After a long day gone, I also have this indelicate desire to be flop free and whip off my bra through my shirt sleeves before I even reach the front door. I may be one of those ladies in the nursing home who gets kicked out due to cussing and creating chaos.

In our house growing up, we got our mouths washed out with soap for swearing. Now when I'm happy, I sputter off innocent words. But when I'm upset, I use the Lord's name in vain, hoping He has a sense of humor when I turn into a foul-mouthed name dropper. I'm not sure where this came from when I was a church going purist who was taught better. In my past I would have said, "Dangit. There's a piece of toilet paper stuck to my behind." Now, I'm exerting every effort to sound off irreverently about whatever experience is annoying me. In order to curb such enthusiasm, I looked into this disturbing characteristic. Seems I have lalochezia, the emotional relief gained from using vulgar language. Then I'm mad at myself and proceed to walk around and do something else that's dumb, experiencing life at the rate of several more profanities per minute. I don't often use big words. Not when a singularly linguistic expression can satisfy my immediate need.

Of course not all females swear. But I have witnessed quite a few using grandiloquent language. The last time I was on an airplane, that lively pedestrian platform that has people watching at its finest, I thought I would be zenning out when in fact I ended up interacting with a collection of female cussers. I sat next to one gal and immediately said to her, "I know it's against code and all, but if we experience any skydiving, I'll adjust your oxygen mask after you adjust mine." She rolled her eyes and started spouting off at me as if I was some kind of self-centered gamine with wicked charm. But I stayed wildly optimistic that she would save my life in case of a dire emergency. She began describing her dislike for airplane food, complaining that it tasted like "f-ing cardboard." Whereas I told her, "There's always peanuts!" Some cheered me on. Although I've known others in my life who have wanted to gag me from day one. She started mumbling a bunch of sentence enhancers that would have made a sailor sound like a saint. It brought to light my own iniquitous and foolish practices of profanity use.

When I turned away, I observed a couple who was obviously on their anniversary trip since he was presenting her with a wrapped box. She wanted one with diamonds in it, but he surprised her with a gift certificate to Victoria's Secret. Every strand on her mood swing snapped, and she possessed a demeanor that suggested she was unsatisfied with his sexual gift. It sounded like they had a successful relationship when I overheard something about four children, five grandchildren, and ten thousand days of togetherness. And I assumed there were zero stabbings during that lengthy time period. But that moment was forever captured with quite a blasphemous retort from the wife that ended with a wonderful exchange. One that almost made me want to be married.

Not fifteen minutes later, a boy was kicking the back of another woman's seat. Meanwhile, the man next to her decided to take a reclining snoozer by taking up two seats to nap. She was not a happy-go-lucky beam of flourishing sunshine. I suppose she began swearing because beating the hell out of two humans is illegal in most states. I cannot repeat what the woman said. I can only say that the younger mister adorableness was a sponge, and that those vocables do not vaporize so quickly. Her words packed a serious punch and he could have repeated them. It was bad enough he called her "meannie head." She erupted again, correcting his comeback while verbally bashing the man next to her with more smuttiness. This might be what happens when you don't pay close attention to your espresso intake. Or I came to another epiphany that maybe she was menopausal and someone messed with the airline thermostat. I do believe that women with that sort of influence usually live longer than men who mention it.

My body language doesn't always say what I'm thinking. But watching this babe told me that she was probably prepared to use a closed fist on both of them while spouting off indecencies. People in the down under know how to react to things like this. Aussies would tell the woman, "That's a bit crikey ya wanker!" Which is the clean way of saying, "Oh my gosh, you idiot." This prolonged stay in verbal punishment prison made me want to chant, "Stop, in the name of love," besides stopping my own profanity use. I knew it was a good day when I didn't need to unleash my own flying innuendos. And I could have, since there is usually a screaming toddler on board, or when you're hedged between two tedious talkers with horrid breath, or when the lavatory is being overly occupied by sex-driven couples. Vulgarities could have easily erupted when the young girl in front of me decided to free her forever flowing hair by letting it drop behind her seat and onto my tray table where my food was resting, not to mention covering my in-flight video and totally blocking those Jerry & Kramer shenanigans. The man on the other side of me recommended that I not point my finger and try to arrange safe words when describing my angst. Lucky for Rapunzel I wasn't carrying any hair cutting shears. I did wonder if the airplane masks that dropped down carried something else besides oxygen.

 I have used the "F" bomb, trying fiercely to change it to "fudge." The problem with that is, I think about food and then run to the store for Fudgsicles and whatever else has crystalline candy and saturated fats in it. As I get older, I realize I should take up other hobbies like knitting. Or muzzle wearing.

Bugged

I had a near death experience when my grown children came to visit and brought to my attention the expired dates on certain refrigerated items. All of a sudden, I was hosting a thoroughly observant couple of killjoys and contemplating my fate. Then again, they care about me. Maybe they care more about what happens to them if I feed them decomposing food products. I can still hear the tutelary deity of edibles to whom I owe my health and happiness. "The mayo was best used before last September. And the soy sauce expired in May 2013." I don't necessarily take on the vapid involvement of watching for expirations on groceries I have stored. Right before bedtime I couldn't help but tell my fellow protesters, "Sleep tight. Don't let the food bugs bite."

I'd just like to say that if I die, I would like some of football's cutest linebackers running to my rescue by taking turns doing mouth to mouth trying to resuscitate me. It stands to reason that if my kitchen contents can make people deathly ill or cause stray animals to come from a five block radius, I suppose I should toss the noxious substances. I've had milk clogging the carton because of curds clumping heavily and cereal sliding out of the box in a solid block. I suppose I stand a better chance of surviving if cheese doesn't show green fuzzy stuff and potatoes don't grow foliage after leaving a long standing stench. Yet there are much bigger threats to worry about than my highly conspicuous consumptions. Like the danger of a communistic takeover of America. It's a well known fact that human guts are filled with bugs and bacteria containing a highly diverse microbial community. Just to be clear, I'm not exactly enchanted at having anything roaming around inside me that will hatch and feed off my organs and central nervous system.

A cheerful enchantress like myself can surely turn into a grumbling kitchen examiner if I have to inspect ingredients in exchange for some pancakes or freshly baked muffins. My dad made the most amazing first meals of the day. And my mother was the ultimate hostess, serving up several of her gourmet goodnesses. I never once saw either of them investigating cupboard or refrigerated contents before cooking. What I saw was two people mumbling vulgarities when there weren't enough eggs or milk in the fridge to cook with unless the recipes called for cracked oval embryos or only a pinch of pumped moo extract. There was never the peril of food perishing when their ten offspring had wet tongues roosting only inches away from their plates and devoured Aunt Jemima and Oscar Mayer the minute they appeared at mealtimes.

It forced such inquisitorial dogma onto a ten-year-old when I had to ask my Dad, "When can I start learning to cook?" Now if it were me, my answer would have been something like, "Well sweetie, let me pass on what my parents told me as a child, thus sustaining sturdy evidence that cooking developed with the emergence of the extinct hominids, who a million years ago began rubbing sticks together when they became ravenous." But since it was dad talking, he replied, "You can start cooking when your sleep deprived mother isn't able to and you don't use the smoke alarms as background music." At the time, I'm sure he thought I would be a fine contributor to family safety if we simply went out and bought doughnuts. He didn't mention that I had to watch for Weevil Knievels doing crazy stunts inside the pantry.

In the interest of keeping a husband, I figured I should learn to champion the methods of menu making. It was better than polishing his hubcaps. But I never thought I would encounter food infestations. The first time I made a citrus salad with dinner, both male and female fruit flies interceded. Their genders were obvious when the male ones rested on the double cheeseburger, and the females landed on the steamy romantic paperback I was reading. My spouse immediately grabbed a butcher knife and heaved it towards his nutritional entree. I remember it clearly because I felt the breeze as it sliced a few hairs off my eyelashes. What can I say. Back then I had the look and bod of Twiggy and the brain of Peg Bundy.

I reassured my mate that a little extra meat wouldn't hurt him, but he insisted that I make him something else. It was a problem since Jimmy Dean, Angus, and T-bone weren't around as substitutions. While my chowhound waited, I pulled out the box of Bisquick to make some perogies and found little moths flying about. My newlywed grabbed a beer, and while ale companies don't bother with expiration dates since they are never going to make it that far, I couldn't help but sing, "Ninety-nine little bugs in the flour, ninety-nine little bugs..." The hubs joined his indignant songstress by concluding, "Take one down while there's larvae around, there'll be two thousand little bugs in the flour!" Then off we went to Denny's, the most beloved name in fine dining. I had to wonder if they housed fruit flies and moths as well.

Caution to anyone else who comes visiting. If you get a hot dog hidden behind ketchup, mustard, relish, onions, and sauerkraut, there might be a slight chance the wieners are spoiled, all because I didn't give the efforts of food watching the same enthusiasm that I give to gardening or sweepstakes entering. I might make funny faces, the kind of goofiness expressed when a woman is waiting for gag reflexes and a home inspection report. Children want to rely on adults for protection and nourishment. Not kill them. I've already asked Santa if he would bring me an automatically eradicating refrigerator this year. I might want to add muzzles for the kids, pending their re-entry and thrills of new expiries. Especially when they find out that I supply some loss in fluoride stability, since the toothpaste perished a year ago.

Two Scents Worth

Now that I've become a keen sharpshooter, no one should be nervous. If I see something crawling up your leg, the Annie Oakley in me can take out the dreadful creature in half a second. Although it's your leg you might want to worry about. I had to learn how to shoot since we have a lawn invader whose rank presence would make even a garbage truck veer away. Just call me the crazy skunk lady. My neighbors did when I aimed straight at them.

One of the foul-smelling scoundrels comes to visit us every night. And believe me, they are nothing like Ipanema girls parading in who are as they say, tall and tan and young and lovely. These varmints are short and partly pale and older and much wiser and repulsive. It doesn't do me a darn bit of good to stop and smell the ranunculus in my garden when there's a strong toxic scent lurking around them. At first, my boyfriend and I looked at each other wondering who passed this strange sort of gas. We did eat something that night for dinner that made the rapid release of some powerful methane and sulfur. What was worse was having a bigger stinker trailing the yard. Wildlife removal and animal control are never around when you need them. So we decided to take matters into our own hands before being at risk for skunk psychosis.

We began plotting our skunk trapping strategies wondering which artillery methods to wield, without resorting to firing off a few hundred flares then basically bombing our back yard. There would be a lot of damage repair and the reinstallation service of laying new sod and planting shrubs all over again, not to mention the spray that would occur during the obliteration. If we use a simple slingshot, chances are that we would miss the piss-cat and snip off some of our cherished blossoms. I thought about borrowing my friend's dog and have a sleepover for scaring purposes. We could bait the black and white weasel with food, but then we'd have a slew of other unwanted guests. Or we could simply trap him in a cage and play some funky music till he died.

There are fifty states, 3.8 million miles of land mass, and one skunk still willing to walk through our valley of death. We opted to go with Plan W. Whip out the BB gun, sit on the patio with a glass of wine, talk in low monotones, wait for the little mephitis to show up, and maim him till he waddles away and warns the rest of his species never to show up at the Walton-Clark household again. In the corporate world, they pay you big bucks to think this way. What we didn't count on was the fact that we ended up drunk as the skunk. When I watched Cape Fear, I didn't think about the unparalleled suspense. I thought about the same vulnerability from the feeling of being dominated, wondering how I would handle that predator. But something told me it wouldn't be near the same type of situation. I'd probably have to kiss my arse goodbye.

The following night, I sorted my contemplation by importance, comfortableness, and my boyfriend's point of view. So in the general relativistic sense, we both found that patience and not raising a stink ourselves was the best way to prepare for the showdown. I was confident that we could handle being local trappers, as long as the thing didn't score a direct hit from fifty paces, rendering us temporarily blind and useless. I had to practice hitting the patio concrete in case this happened. But if there's one thing I know about striped animals, they don't really come when you call them. My boyfriend reassured me that the long lost and possibly rabid intimidator would want to search our lawn for grubs sooner or later. We sat the next night waiting again while I practiced soberism along with my shooting, trying to keep my trigger happy self under control. I didn't want to sing, really. Singing leads to dancing and possibly spooking the skunk, dancing might lead to me falling and missing out on the actual annihilation, and the skunk might spray me so I'd have to remove all my clothes. Falling might lead to hurting myself and then paramedics would show up and smell my body that would be more noxiously fragrant than a septic tank. Not to mention they would see me naked. After all that Einstein-ish brain activity, the stinkpot decided to take the night off.

    We still haven't caught the odorous animal. But we haven't given up. We have a whole new plan of attack tonight, unless the fur handling auction committee that I called comes to take him away. I was hoping to reveal a fun and final chapter to our skunk saga. Instead, I can only reveal the story my neighbor told me about the time when he dealt with a similarly sly little bugger. Trying to stay incognito since the police station was close by, he grabbed his shotgun, proceeded out the back door where he targeted the perpetrator, fired the carbine, and massacred the unpleasant munchkin with a bang that was heard for miles, ran back into the house and laid down the gun, then nonchalantly walked out the back door again yelling, "What the hell was that?"

    I wouldn't be able to do that. In terms of blatant animal killing, I wouldn't be able to shoot any creature whatsoever. It would make me a very bad person. Besides, skunks chase away summons servers, Jehovah's Witnesses, and sketchy looking people in general.

Cautionary Tales

My beau and I are doing everything in our power to stay alive. We might increase our chances considerably if we never leave the house. Sometimes we sit in front of the television taking one anxiety attack at a time when watching commercial ads that try to sell us supplements for our aging bodies that might just result in dangerous disparity as well. With all their product liabilities and my atrocious luck, I'd probably choke to death trying to swallow their publicized pills. Those ads certainly don't let us sit very comfortably when they are warning: "Don't take if you're a marmot, pregnant, almost pregnant, have been pregnant, prone to sudden bursts of tears, or have moles." And, "At the first sign of paralysis, call your doctor immediately." My mate asked how he could possibly make that call if he's paralyzed.

As we sit in quiet bemusement, we can't help but wonder what's the worst that could happen if we took these questionable capsules? I would probably find a forest and lie on the ground exploring the stars and the deep dark galaxy in broad daylight, during bear mating season. The last time I took something that had significant side effects was about eight years ago. I was walking down the street where I saw a sign on a building and swore it said, "Do not enter or trespassers will be prostituted." I wasn't sure if I should be an example to others and not go in, or prove to myself that my body was still worthy. Because the heavier side effects that day could have been tricking, possible prostitution, jail time, and loss of family and close friends. That was one excited corner of crowded onlookers who were hoping I would drop everything and play strip poker or dance the hip-hop-boob-and-fanny-flop. Meanwhile, my boyfriend at the time didn't take anything and still experienced side effects. Just viewing a picture of Jessica Alba in a bathing suit resulted in uncontrollable manliness. I needed to find something that would settle his horny self down.

When you think about it, there are impending dangers to everything. I refrain from jogging because according to every episode of CSI, there's a big chance I'll run across a dead body. And with all the child protective warnings, it would have been easier just to get rid of my kids. When my middle daughter was small, I was very much aware of warning labels. For one of her playdates, I bought that moldable silicone based substance called Silly Putty which comes in original, glow-in-the-dark, glitter, and four bright colors. Yet the stuff contains colorants that could cause serious side effects of staining, and direct contact can make it stick to hair, batten down eyelashes, and be used as permanent ear and nose plugs when dried. Of course during that lovely little incident, my daughter's girlfriend's mother came over and saw what my darling did to her child. She had been a delightful woman in the past, until she asked if my daughter was a demon. She also inquired what I fed her child for lunch. She gave me the full facts and folklore about hot dogs claiming the meat is simply manslaughter. Little did she know the girls washed their weenies down with 100% healthy fruit juice.

To calm this woman's nerves, I offered her a hefty glass of 100% fruit-stomped juice known as wine. But she said the Surgeon General insists that drinking violaceous substances can result in having headaches so bad that we will want to scoot to the hospital for brain scans. She went on to tell me the other un-dietary side effects that include devouring copious amounts of bar nuts, besides poisoning the bloodstream and explaining all the seventy made up reasons why country singers chant about love gone wrong. I almost drowned myself that day from the goblet filled tsunami of fermented relief. I turned to her teasingly and warned her, "Don't try this at home!" After they left, I ended up reading a book to my daughter about Alice's titillating adventures in a Wonderbra. She read one to me called *Are You My Mother?*

Some memories still come so vividly to me. Many moons ago I housesat for someone who left whimsical warnings throughout his manly shack. The comical and jocose gentleman must have had a jolly time writing me those notes. I went to use the bathroom and found one near the toilet that read, "This area might be lethally hazardous. But zip-a-dee-doo-dah zip-a-dee-ay, just walk away and have yourself a wonderful day!" I should have married the guy. Not for his poor cleaning skills, but for his farcical talents. The gun owner even made his own warning label that read, "Not only will this weapon maim you if you mess with it, it'll hurt the whole time you're dying." Even the washing machine had the warning, "Nothing over fifteen pounds." Only a moron would try to wash the dog in a front loader. The next note was far less convincing. I proceeded to do his wash and a shirt label advised, "For best results, wash in cold water and tumble dry on low heat." If I had been a laundering extremist, I would have been going for the worst results by tying the garment to the top of my car and driving it through the car wash, then drying it by speeding through town at two hundred miles per hour.

But doing that could easily cause injury, frivolous lawsuits, or early onset mortality.

What if we are all forced to wear warning labels? I'm fairly certain mine would caution that I'm known to spontaneously combust and spew liquids, and I shouldn't be left unsupervised under a full moon... or with Italian men. God forbid if I ever have a suffocation warning attached to me that says: "Keep this bag away from babies, pets, and alcohol."

Patty Clark

Worn like sacred badges of honor

When You Wish Upon a Star

In an unexpected moment of devotion, my doting boyfriend came up to me and said, "I love you." I asked "Why?" He responded, "I don't know. I haven't figured that out yet." I don't always whimper. But when I do, questionable fondness is probably involved. But I am convinced that this man adores me so much that he would never use me as bait on a safari if it were a choice between him and me in a tiger attack. I like to be the reason he smiles when he knows he's going to get eaten alive. Here is another endearing phrase he uses. "Every breath you take, every move you make, I'll be watching you." But the relationship will continue to grow and prosper and mutually benefit both of us, if he doesn't stand over me with a pillow and a gun when I snore.

Speaking of such profound adoration, both my Dad and my boyfriend think Sophia Loren is simply the sexiest woman ever. I have often wondered, out of the millions of women on earth, why Sophia? Is it the curvaceous figure? Or the fact that she wows a crowd with her movie star glamour? Is it the charcoal winged eyeliner she so pointedly paints above and below her eyes that extends almost to her earlobes and screams "Here I am, boys!" People may not recognize me anymore once I start penciling in wickedly black and lengthy enhancers. But I suspect the good Lord did not intend for men to ogle over just one woman.

Recently my beau and I stayed in a Hollywood hotel where every elevator is plastered with life-sized movie stars. You walk into one and cannot help but become enchanted by the famous highnesses of Hollywood who have you mesmerized when they stare into your eyes. After a night of moderate drinking, we proceeded back to our hotel where Loverboy and I entered one of the big square hoists, and he immediately zooms in on the female stars. "Hey girls," he says followed with "nevermind." As if they weren't exactly the girls he wanted to flirt with. I asked him, "What about Marilyn?" He answered, "Nope. It's gotta be Sophia Loren." We walked down the hall to our room that was lined with more photographs of classic stars. I mosied by each one, pointing out Greta Garbo, Montgomery Clift, Veronica Lake, and Lawrence Olivier. Then I yelled, "No way! They placed Sophia Loren right next to OUR room?? What are the odds!" I'm not normally a jealous woman. But I was in star hell that night having to share my beau with a classic Italian pin-up actress, listening to the kind of coquetry carried on by my lover and the sexy Sophia. Her smirky smile threatened to reduce me to something very much like a creature from another planet. Is it a coincidence that I brought along my current reading material *Why Men Die First*? I'm sure there are chapters coming up about crushes, homewreckers, infidelity, and perhaps bloodshed.

Sure, it could have been the three glasses of wine. But I had to explain to my sweet sugardumpling that when a woman wants a guy, first she has to make sure he isn't with another woman. Then she should catch his eye and hold his gaze for five seconds. I'd say the sultry Sophia was holding his gaze the entire time we stood there talking. Then a woman is supposed to flip her hair and walk away. I tried telling mister stud muffin that women who can't flip their hair and walk away are needy and can clamp onto a guy like a bloodthirsty parasite. I've done more research on domestic intelligence than the FBI, and sometimes the smallest step of reassurance can activate the mightiest of miracles. I wondered if the aging star suffers like I do from memory loss, and if she too disguises her midriff. In fact, I wanted to go home and look into the dilapidated factors of other famous women. I tried gaining his attention back by laughing at his sleek lady-killer impersonation, and restructuring the conversation towards something a little more intriguing like the Louisiana Purchase. After all, I'm no stranger to wine's magical powers myself. I was almost sure I heard the urbane actress offer my guy a lovely lap dance.

No wonder my beau was so amorous that night. He burst into the room and grabbed me passionately. He claims it's not about sex with Sophia. It's more about sensuality. Even though I knew our love would burn stronger than a wired tungsten filament in a see through bulb, I wasn't born yesterday, or the day before that. I'd be lying if I said I didn't stay awake that night wondering about the women he dreams about. At about four in the morning I told him, "Honey, it's been three years now. I think it's time we seriously thought about cutting ties to past loves."

Women want trust, loyalty, affection, and no gaping at other gals. Then we will do most anything men want, except move to a remote fishery in the Yukon. As we left the room to check out, my fella said, "I'm walking right by her since I only have eyes for you babe." That was special. I think crazy girlfriends are the best because you never know what you're going to get. You might get eight hours of solid sleep yourself—or be awakened by a slinging of catcalls by your mate who swears she is Batwoman but looks more like a disheveled Bride of Chucky on some mission to murder somebody. I usually need seven hours of healthful beauty sleep. Ten if I'm deplorable.

According to Sir Jiminy Cricket, when you wish upon a star, it makes no difference who you are and your dreams come true. I thought maybe the rapturous Sophia was going to come down off the wall and have her way with my man. If that had been the case, I would have been searching that wall for Cary Grant.

It's my Party and I'll Cry if I Need to

♥

We had just recovered from New Year's when my boyfriend decided to throw a celebration of my natal day. He was discussing everything from attendees to my cake of choice. Now half the state of California is coming. It started out with just family. Then a few friends, most of which are HIS friends. I think he tried inviting a few famous football players. He even wanted to invite the waiter at the last restaurant where we dined. He finally trimmed it down to a stadium full and did indeed think that a sports arena would be the most suitable place to host this party. I told him, "You know love buns, you can keep your sporting events on the whole time we are trying to enjoy your guests." After a lifetime and an exceptional male-minded education, I'm probably the only woman ever known to browse game times on her birthday.

With this many people attending, I politely suggested, "Costco has great cake batter. Maybe we should get a sheet cake." It was my funny man's moment to out-humor me when he responded, "I'll HAVE to get one to hold THAT many candles!" If I didn't know better, I'd swear I was dating Billy Crystal. He'll probably get a frozen cake, which is basically a box of popsicles. But I'm a Capricornial goat, unafraid to break traditions and try new things. The only thing that could improve my party enthusiasm is if he walked in with a ten-tiered decadent devil's food confection topped with chunks of chocolate and dribbled with fudge, and out jumps Tom Brady. Because size with a prize does matter.

My squeeze, who took his role as a party planner rather seriously, and who also wanted to show off his BBQing skills, said he wanted to smoke some baby back ribs all day. That is until he realized his smoker wouldn't hold the entire ribcage of a pig. He was about to order slabs from his favorite meat market when he found out they were closed for renovations. It wouldn't befit the griller to embrace the simplicity of bologna sandwiches, or just leave a lot of peanuts lying around. Nor is the Capricorn very picky about such incidentals (ahem). She'd be happy just drinking most of her dinner anyway.

What's another birthday when you're already showing all the signs of deterioration. We've timed it now. It takes both my beau and I exactly fourteen minutes to pull up Netflix streaming with their library of videos. Not to mention the fact that we can't see which buttons to push on different operational devices, one of which is connected to Playstation. I don't want my entertainment to be anywhere associated with Marvel Super Heroes vs Streetfighters. He doesn't know it yet, but I got him a present for my birthday. It's a universal large-font remote.

I am consumed yearly with taking all those anti-aging pills. When walking around with ballooning bags under my eyes, I take double. But if I'm to have a fabulous birthday, I need to forget the age factor. Let my boobies fall where they may. But I'll need all the strength and actability I can accumulate to blow out my candles. I certainly want most of my wishes to come true. I do realize that it's far better being over the hill than a few feet under it. It's a day of reflection, as long as it's not through a mirror. Capricorns aren't characteristically callous though if you push me right to the edge, I'm not the one going over. My belief in astrology is inversely proportional to my planetary positioning. It basically means that I don't know where the heck I'm going from here.

Birthdays are one day closer to finding out if there are really heavenly beings and pearly gates and a divine leader and if my Grandpa and Amy Winehouse are really behind them. And, if worms will eventually digest my decomposing Donna Karan designs as I rot away in a funerary chamber. If cremated and scattered, I do hope my ashes blow towards the northern end of Los Angeles. Santa Barbara is an awfully nice place to sit and rest. Birthdays are also one day closer to Depends. Because if this party is anything like our New Year's Eve bash, there will be three times the jokes and laughter forcing me to dampen my derriere.

Back to the party attendees, because I don't plan on kicking the bucket till well after my party. I suggested no presents, just the presence of anyone who needed something to do that day. And in return, all they had to do was leave the house slightly cleaner than when they got there. As it turned out, eighteen people took off before I could say thanks for the memories. Six brought me a card. Twelve wanted to get me a card but didn't have time to stop at a store. A number of them just wanted to see me. Most of them just wanted to see me loaded. All the others didn't know who I was but wished me a happy birthday anyway.

I asked God to grant me the serenity to accept another year, the courage to go further into my sixties, and the wisdom to know the difference between good ultra-lift, anti-wrinkle firming creams and ones that are rip-offs. And as they say, I need to forget about what I've done in the past because I can't change it. I need to forget about the future when I can't predict it. And I should forget about all those presents I could have received if I had kept my mouth shut since I told people not to bring any. Birthdays come. Birthdays go. I've learned to cosmeticize, acclimatize, tranquilize, and allow myself all the great advantages of being over sixty. I'm still active, and I sure can make a mean pitcher of martinis. So technically, I can add "Mixing & Blending Machine Operator" to my resume. I pruned our macadamia tree, which also allows me the position of "Branch Manager" somewhere. I put on a bra every day, so I can be documented as a "Rack Loader" with still some slight growth potential. There are benefits to birthday girls like me. I'm an awesome cuddler, and I will give other people presents on my birthday like sharing my cocktails. And I promise not to let tears fall into my cake.

Mom Always Liked Me Least

Everyone knows by now that I come from a family of very familiar faces since there were twelve of us jammed into seventeen hundred square feet of communal living. Not to mention cousins and friends who made appearances. Thunder only happens when it's raining relatives and rambunctious outsiders. Before my Mother Hubbard was a woman living in a shoe box fetching her munchkins chow, she was a fourteenth century Indian princess. I know this because I resided with tribal life forms who continued to specialize in warfare, and I too waited for storms to pass.

Mom must have liked me the least when she started confusing me with the nanny we didn't have, and giving me the privilege of babysitting, tot sitting, adolescent sitting, pet sitting, and sitting for whoever was over at the time. There was an increase in atmospheric pressure when up against tail winds of romping, stomping, and vociferous siblings. I started to suspect that the tonality of such sounds had been specifically calibrated to annoy me. They took all the fun out of my sitting around eating Oreos in peace and quiet. I couldn't even enjoy Oreos, or food period. Not with ravenous youngsters around who were diminishing pantry and refrigerator contents hourly. One time they ate all the ice cream. I screamed, they screamed, we all screamed, and the police came. It was awkward. Next to the circus, there wasn't anything that generated excitement quite like being entrusted with hungry clowns and animals when my mother was gone and having the cops show up. Mom taught me that a woman has to become an expert delegator and ringmaster, but every performance skill requires some potent form of pandemonium relief. Now I see why she downed gobs of Chablis.

God must have created toilets for the times a younger brother decides to wash cast iron cookware. I guess it beat looking at Highlights magazine or being entertained by Sesame Street. Though God did not take into consideration the steady stream of water that follows a tank breakage. He should have also constructed a dam to prevent the marshy liquid from colliding with the carpeting and wood floors. Then I freaked out when my baby brother pulled the toilet paper all the way into the garage, then sat there eating it. I cleaned his mouth out while our sister was shoving pennies into her kisser. By the time another sibling filled his jaw with jelly beans, I figured it was probably unnecessary to feed any of them lunch. When I did pump out sandwiches, you would have thought I was repetitively competing with an assembly linewoman at a food processing plant.

My sister, Miss Enchanted with antenna'd electronics, decided to rise and shine long enough to turn on her favorite form of telly amusement, while our youngest sister finger painted the walls, pedicured her stuffed animals, pranced around naked wearing nothing but oven mitts and Mom's favorite high heels, called Venezuela, finished the Times crossword puzzle with Crayolas, and was still bored stiff. I have long felt that I was never meant to be domesticated. Don't get me wrong. I love kids as long as they are still cooing. There was no doubt that babysitting my siblings was pure preparation for motherhood. It's a wonder I ever had children myself and didn't limit my tender care to pint-sized pets with castrated vocal chords. I would have been better off putting the kids in our pet cages and letting the pets run free.

Day care duties were almost always interrupted by bell-ringing sales people, but my parents told me never answer the door to strangers. Solicitors really risked their lives if my two older brothers were anywhere in the vicinity with sling shots aimed at icicles that lined our front sidewalk. Mom arrived home just in time to fall on broken frozen crystals, and to see a snowman wearing her scarf and expensive pearls. One of her offspring did a self-barbered butcher job while another was coaxing a fat wad of chewed gum from the bathroom faucet. My teens were smarter than that. They used their allowance to go to a beauty salon to get fantastic asymmetrical shaved hairdos with purple highlights. And they didn't stuff gum into faucets. But they did plug up the toilet on several occasions with Kotex pads. Yet I didn't want to indoctrinate my own children into a system that doesn't value creative expression or discourages their competence. But they did wonder why I never bought gum.

It was hard keeping track of so many characters in my mother's absence. The minute she got home she asked, "Where are all your sisters and brothers?" I recall crossing off the childcare checklist by telling her, "Well, let me see. The last time I looked, Eddie Munster and Pugsley Addams were outside digging Marsha Brady out of piled snow. Cindy Brady is blowing polish dry on her doll's toes. Opie Taylor was pulling popcorn out from under the couch cushions and storing them in his sock. I think he might be a squirrel. Gidget has her boyfriend over in the bedroom. Hopefully Will Robinson isn't under any impending danger of drowning. He went to the lake and has been warned about falling through thin ice. Dennis the Menace is being very sportsmanlike playing darts with Lassie, although I left him the board and took away the small steel missiles for safekeeping. And right before Huck Finn was sucking gum from the faucet with the vacuum cleaner, he was having a private moment in the tropics, heating up the place by playing with matches. Not to worry though. I called the fire department and urged them to be on standby."

The hardest part of babysitting was having my mother criticize my temporary custody capabilities. It's funny how her eye-rolling was so similar to that of my siblings. She had to wonder again about me when I lay down next to the dog explaining why I wasn't his biological babysitter.

Blah Blah Blah

Ecclesiastes says that there is a season for every activity under heaven. A time to be born, a time to die, a time to figure out what the heck I'm going to do with myself in between. It's January. A month of listlessness and prevailing boredom. The kids have gone home. Credit card bills will start pouring in from Christmas, and I might get off a whole lot cheaper if I just change my address. I have already failed my New Year's resolutions somewhere between nine and noon. And I need vagus nerve stimulation. If I want to start out the Year feeling somewhat optimistic, I should probably begin with several milligrams of Paxil.

To ward off boredom, I accelerated my respiratory system by breathing in and out till I got dizzy. I replaced every powering device in my household with a fresh round of batteries. It took me an hour to figure out if blue or green was my favorite color. I can always lie in the hammock and take a long winter's nap waiting for spring, or clean something. There are chores that start over again the minute I complete them. I cast a rapid glance at all those in the room and grabbed those pencils placing them in a cup by pointing them in the same direction at the same time I was talking to the lead filled sticks. "I'll bet you're all wondering why I gathered you here today!" Heaven forbid if we have an earthquake. The etch-a-sketch portrait of myself will get ruined.

I did stand at the sink full of dishes watching my dry cracked fingers prune as I gathered more ideas on how to have a good time. Thankfully, my granddaughter called. I told her that she should have motivating New Year's resolutions. "Be helpful, drink more water, and marry Adam Lambert." After that, I grabbed my phone and took a snapshot of my last meal and sent it to everyone as if they have never seen guacamole dip before. I could change my car horn to the sound of fireworks. Or I could ponder the problems of mutation. Except the Neanderthals did it and they're all dead. Every one of them. A massage would feel good. Then it dawned on me, I'm out of ice cubes. I refuse to dissect ants on moral grounds. But the devil intervened and tried coercing me into becoming mischievously unprincipled by texting random numbers expressing, "I offed the guy. Now what am I supposed to do with the body?" I called down legions of angels to rescue me from executing that idea. Although temporarily amusing, I knew after four hours of doing it that I would just be bored again. I've been meaning to conduct myself with more practical expediency. But there are too many other rousing options.

If my mother were alive, she would tell me, "Go find something to do!" Not wanting my cortisol levels to go down, I decided to run outside garnering enough photosynthesis from the sun's luminous veil of light to turn it into nutrition for my body that basically might keep me from getting vehemently depressed. After filling ice cube trays, I watched *Ferris Bueller* who stolidly declared, "Life moves pretty fast. If you don't stop and look around once in awhile, you could miss it." I looked around. All I saw was a basket overflowing with dirty laundry. I decided to take the day off myself from doing anything stressful that could result in static electricity, sending mild charges to my system since I'm out of dryer sheets.

Ferris made me realize that I'm a righteous dudette. Although the sportos, the motorheads, the geeks, sluts, wasteoids, and dweebies don't adore me and could care less who I am or what I'm doing. My computer soon summoned, making me Google movie stars. Specifically, Mark Wahlberg's brachii muscles. It was about the same time I was thinking what I'll have for lunch tomorrow and if I should diet. Come to find out, Mark stays in top shape for films then rewards himself. Pancakes, double dough pepperoni pizzas, and brownies with a huge mug of milk. If I rewarded myself with that much food, I would be resting for a lengthy period within the confines of a coffin. Although I do find it's impossible to experience happiness unless I'm gorging on the weight inducing blissfullness of anything that isn't good for me.

Which brings me to fitness. Thus far, I haven't been too inclined to diet. Now I'm into gut jiggling. The most calories I've burned was the apple crisp I forgot was in the oven when I went outside to pick weeds. Back in 1991, I lost 7.3 pounds, but that was with my third newborn. I'd lose twenty-four more pounds per year if I stopped eating those three gallon tubs of premium ice cream and probably seventy more pounds if I ran around the block every day with my neighbors Irish setter. So much for entering the Olympics. I'm on my third cupcake. I spent the entire holiday season running myself ragged and exercising every part of my body. So I'm giving up any sort of physical activity for Lent, starting now. Anyway, my insurance doesn't handle body splints. The only way I'll get to be smokin' hot is in a fiery tunnel turning my body to ashes when I'm dead.

I'd like to take a moment of silence to observe the stair stepper, that mega metal of resistance and severe boredom unidentifiable to my aging and senescent physique. Personally, I'd like to observe twelve months of treading silence and not spend one micro-second on a machine that makes me hold on for dear life. Where some see body building, I see sweating, over stimulation, and general nausea. There are far better ways to trick my body into releasing oxytocin. Who's with me? Or we could play *Hunger Games* and see who comes out of that alive. Furthermore, let's all take a moment of silence for all those younger parents who cannot take a moment for either exercise or silence, since they have toddlers.

Life is mesmerizing. Eat. Sleep. Poop. Try not to be bored. Which makes it even more entrancing when I can't stop thinking about vacations and retirement.

Patty Melt

For years I envisioned the prospect of empty nesting with popping corks and practically packing my girls bags for them. As it turned out, cutting the cords was slightly more difficult than planned. I find myself wanting to walk the neighbor's Yorkie in the old baby buggy. Sometimes I will even turn on Barney just for old time's sake or become a burgeoning storyteller for ravens. I sway back and forth while surveying greeting cards in store aisles as if I'm holding a newborn, being mistaken for a person with quite the conspicuous need to pee. A lady approached me recently pointing out the restroom then shook her head wondering why I still stood there pendulating.

Unless I got their meanings wrong, songsters everywhere have revealed their feelings from their own parental points of view. The Fifth Dimension was fairly accurate. I now have "one less phone call to answer, one less egg to fry, one less child to pick up after." But Bonnie Tyler said it more appropriately. "It's nothing but a heartache, hits you when it's too late." I'd say Bonnie's words relate better to both the empty nest, and bulging bladders.

I am free to be me and eat bonbons for breakfast. And my chances of being stricken with germophobic illnesses have declined immensely, not to mention medical costs have dwindled. None of that matters though when you miss your offspring once they're gone. Up until now, I had never heard "blackbirds singing in the dead of night." I find myself crushing up bags of Corn Curls and spreading them into the couch cushions then eating the crumbs as a reminder of messes my kids made. And I don't even like Corn Curls. I would give anything these days to have the unceasing whirlwind of activity, or a cold contracted by bacterial ridden tykes. At least we'd be in bed together snuggling in the luxurious folds of my new magnificent linens, fighting over the remote control. I remember when their rapping radios almost did me in. But I would love a chance to say "put another dime in that jukebox baby." I was ready to kill anyone who gave my girls a play piano, or any other insufferable deafening device for that matter. There was a passionate place inside of me that used to vocalize, "QUUIIIEEETTT!!!" At one point I recall thinking to myself, "Slow down, you move too fast. Got to make the mornings last." I wasn't feelin' too groovy then, and I'm not feelin' all that groovy now. I would be "glad all over" having bedlam again, especially now that my hearing is fading away.

My first granddaughter just came for a visit, and I hadn't had that much excitement since the D'Arcys blew up the Bundy household with a rocket launcher on *Married With Children*. During my grandsweeties stay, I was generously awarded with another new grandbaby. Bound by her irresistibility, I feel very much the same way as the Kinks do when they sing, "Girl I want to be with you, all of the time, all day, and all of the night." It doesn't seem that long ago when I was telling each of my offspring, "Ooh-oo child, things are gonna get easier." Now they should be singing that to me. I really wouldn't want to parent again any more than I would want to wrestle a steer in a rodeo. But as the crooning Bryan Adams belts out, "Those were the best days of my life"... aside from the coupla sessions as a lounge singer when I was soused on margaritas.

Quoting Reba McIntyre, you need three things in life. A wishbone, a backbone, and a funny bone. Hopefully my daughters will have all three if I ever decide to take turns living with each of them. After all, grandmothers are "a little bit parent, a little bit teacher, and a little bit rockin and rollin" from all the parenting and teaching. But I have garnered a veritable vault of maternal wisdom, and my girls should know that we are people who watch the kids carefully instead of watching the television. I do promise not to retain the unfailing eagerness to intercede or hunt them down like a bloodhound when they aren't home on time. It's like I told each and every one of them throughout their residency at my maison. "We'll be swell roommates as long as you don't leave anything out of place and you let me sleep at night." It's good to have those binding covenants. They may still need to know how to cut a pineapple, or learn that the sum of the square roots of any two sides of an isosceles triangle is equal to the square root of the remaining side. I doubt they paid that much attention to mathematics while we watched *The Wizard of Oz*. Besides, living together will be all laughs until I actually laugh and wet my pants.

After my first born, I remember needing my mother and called her frantically for help. "Hi Mom. It's Patty, your oldest daughter. I'm making Beef Stroganoff and Snickerdoodles for guests and haven't the time to run to the store. Is there a substitution for molasses? She answered, "Tupelo, honey!" Then I asked if there was a substitution for beef. She said, "Yes. Eight vegetables." Jesting most certainly inhabited the genes. But she reassured me many times, "You is kind. You is smart. You is important." I wasn't sure if I dialed my mother, or Viola Davis.

One element of torture is encapsulating this journey with not much say in matters of visitation. Hopefully my girls won't live as far as Abu Dhabi, or bolt their doors when I show up. Which would literally put me somewhere between rocks and a hard place (grave). I'd hate to be "standing in the shadows of love" with dewy eyes. I realize their lives are busy. But I must have confidence that my girls "will still need me and feed me when I'm eighty-four" with something a bit more satisfying than pureed spinach.

It's an echoing sentiment I know, but my aorta melts when I see my kids and grandkids. Mothers are programmed to maintain blood flow to their hearts by staying actively stimulated chasing children. So it feels like I have unfinished business to attend to. Yet I suppose a prime measure of maturity would be to suck up this empty nest affliction and salubriously move on.

Liberating myself from mental slavery

Cursed

It was my eighteenth year of living when I honestly thought I was going to be the next Virgin Mary. The nuns of holy agony pried me away from any boy that came within touching distance and made me guilt ridden for years. I had to sit in a dimly lit church confessional expressing every transgression to a shadowed ecclesiastic. Then I averaged two icy plunges per week into holy water. In my eyes, those lusts and excesses were not so despicable, and I shouldn't have had such harsh penances like a million Hail Marys. The priest never understood the severity of my suffering. It's not like I robbed the church basket or threw a baby bunny off a bridge. Although I admit to leaving urine specimens in swimming pools and having my parents cater to my long lists of demands. Unlike most mischievous girls, Marie Antoinette never knew the adolescent amusement of teepeeing the neighbor's house with multi-hued crepe paper, right before it rained. Neither did I. But I can't say that I didn't think about it.

Now I'm only 15% Catholic, and I don't consider my sins scarlett anymore. They are more on the pinkish side. I spent countless Sundays going to the altar, eating a wafer and gulping some wine, going home with an overwhelming desire to do something a bit naughty. I mean when a pastor invites me to eat flesh and drink blood, I thought it was a forum for cannabilism. And I was forced to give up things like doughnuts for Lent. I would have liked it more if the communion wafers had been satisfyingly smothered in caramel and colored sprinkles and the wine was 100% Welch's. And church attendance would have risen substantially if Clive Owen had been my pastor.

Week after week, I found myself cowering before the clergyman. "Father, I know it's only been fifteen minutes since my last confession. But will I be forgiven for singeing my sister's hair with the matches that I wasn't supposed to play with?" I began to sense the monumental amount of guilt that I was going to feel for the rest of my impish existence. But I must have done something right. When I was a pre-teen, I entered a contest for a bike and won. Then I gave it to my girlfriend who needed it more than I did. That same week I found myself back in the confessional repenting, "Bless me Father for I have stained the carpeting while chasing the dog." According to my mother, it was a sin to be in hot pursuit of someone while holding an open container of chocolate milk. I'd like to clear my conscience completely about all those supposedly horrible things I did that sent me into a deep shameful spiral and has haunted me until 1998. That's the year I began living guilt free. But what if I'm playing baseball and I steal second base? Does that count? And I want to know who exactly carved out those Commandments? "Thou shall not take the name of the Lord your God in vain." I believe that saying "Jesus" beats the "F" word. And "Thou shall not make idols," unless I want to buy beer for the under-aged and have them worship me forever after. I did learn that thou shall not make large bank withdrawals with a loaded weapon. And to "love thy neighbor," even though I'm not a fan of their fourteen garden gnomes.

My parents should have joined Compulsive Liars Anonymous with all the sandbagging they dispensed, like telling us that Santa was living large and somewhere north with flying reindeer. I eventually took on the hobby of habitual lying myself. Like the big bad bear in the kitchen lie. I told my girls that if they held the freezer door open too long the cold would get out and a huge polar bear might appear. My animal loving middle daughter stood in front of the appliance long enough to catch pneumonia telling me, "I'm just waiting to hug the big guy."

I was also culpable for hiding my children's toys that were deadly obstacles and obnoxiously loud. "Gee, I'm not exactly sure where your Barbie shoes and Mr. Microphone are!" So it's no wonder each of my girls at one time or another fibbed, "I haven't seen your lipstick," when clearly their mouths all the way to their earlobes drastically displayed the colored cosmetic. I wondered how old they were before they realized that "Mommy and Daddy were just doing gymnastics in the bedroom" was a great big crock of sham. I had to explain that saying "Oh God" wasn't showing disrespect to the Lord in any way just because we weren't in church. It was worth every flame of eternal hellfire that awaits my wicked body.

It was bad enough repenting for my own misdeeds. I also found myself praying on behalf of a contrite child. "Bless her Father, for she has strayed into the Miller's yard and picked all their begonias." Not to mention my girls' concocting fictional stories for the neighbors about us never having any groceries in the house when I practically took out food loans to feed them. All those times I took them to Chuck-E-Cheese for dinner eventually led to guilt. I thought that establishing lousy nourishment and teaching them how to pass off counterfeit coins while I was chugging beer was a grand idea at the time. Once I forgot to leave tooth money under one daughter's pillow and had to come up with a fast thinking fabrication that the fairy only comes on second Saturdays of the month. I thought my words would be richly flavored with trust and thankfulness. But no. Now that my girls are adults, they can't ask me anything anymore without counting on the validity of a polygraph test.

After inhabiting this planet for over half a century, I've experienced random flashes of light that could either be the Lord speaking to me, or the mere warning to run for cover in a lightning storm. In order to become more of an immaculate me, I shouldn't have to say, "Bless me Father for I have slaughtered" every time I stomp out a centipede. And I suppose I should be truthful when someone asks if I dye my hair. Had my mother been a more intimately connected with Conan O'Brien, I'd be a genuine redhead. When I end up in a senior home and raise my hand to use the bathroom, I hope they won't think I'm lying when I say, "I really have to go."

Goddess of Recreation

My employment gives me a lot of freedom. I am a work-from-home assistant, high and holy baroness, and queenly executive who likes to find alternate things to do rather than slaving away. I wake at nine, some days more punctually at ten. Certain liberties have been taken into consideration when it comes to my dress code. My standard uniform consists of a T-shirt, leggings, and no make-up with sloppy hair naturalness. I take my mid-morning break, then lunch at eleven-fifteen, and rush back around four. This may surprise you, but I work rather diligently. Except for those times I feel the quantum stealth of anonymousness, and I'm off doing something a little more intriguing.

Thankfully I'm not required to do anything inventorial, janitorial, or sit in a patent office every day, angst ridden for not brainstorming some of the business ideas myself. My boss is pretty much the only person who doesn't view me as an idiot. Although, he has never seen me sitting on a bar stool talking like a damn fool. The best part of waking up is having whatever I want in my cup, and not having to get dressed. I spend half the day wondering if it's too late to drink coffee and the other half wondering if it's too early for happy hour.

When my bossyman tells me to have a nice day, I figure he means to harness any fear of determination and do what pleases me. And what pleases me is not having continuous confinement. At the same time, he does wield the power to rattle my erudite mind by wanting me to perform certain duties. But instead of sitting at home thinking about windsurfing, I would much rather stand on a sailboard in the glorious outdoors and think about my beloved employer. Blame it on the basophilic granules surrounding my hippocampal neurons. My doctor says that I have a terminal condition with only another thirty years to live. So I'd like to make the most of it. I'm blemished perhaps. Unfinished for sure.

Life has brought peaceful change to both my work and motherly duties. I can sit quietly in my home knowing it will stay fairly clean and I won't have to cover the furniture in plastic unless I become increasingly incontinent. What I remember most about having kids at home was that their presence tended to disarrange my revered ecosystem. There were also those little known dangers of Barbie accessories that can leave lasting impressions in one's soles. Now, it's only the crow's feet I have to worry about. My floppy frontal lobes won't be under scrutiny since I'm in a more private place of employment. I have jettisoned my torturous high heels and elastic burdening by tossing my bra aside during servitude. And what's interesting, I get along famously with everyone in my office now. Although my boyfriend came into my work space yesterday and nudged me asking, "Sorry to bother you, but I was wondering if you are Sleeping Beauty and it's your day off." Except that Sleeping Beauty was ravishing. My appearance resembles the unglamorized Martha Stewart during her stint in a holding cell.

There are only a few things that would take me far away from my work. Jury duty. A flight to Figi. Store bargains. A massage. Terroristic threats. Rain in Spain. The list goes on. I have to keep in mind that I cannot use the excuse during truancy that my uncle died if I'm going to forget that I already used that excuse five times.

My employer may have thought it was a bit scamming of me the day I called saying I was sprayed by a skunk. He had no way of verifying it. How do I know that he himself isn't possibly bipolar with subtle hints of body odor? When I was employed as a teen, I had a written excuse that I was bitten by a rabid, blood thirsty bullhound and signed it, Dr. Zhivago. I also used the excuse one time that my Chicano brother was kidnapped by the drug cartel in Mexico. Born a blonde, I wanted to see how long it took my boss to realize what nationality I was.

Since I work from home, I notice more things now. Cracks in the ceiling. Our parrot's tooth decay. How much I love Home Town Buffets at home. Plans for this afternoon may include driving to Target for more food and switching out their rose scented deodorants for spring meadow. Although I should probably keep in mind that thirty million fingers are lost yearly due to people touching other people's things. There's always drunk-in-the-middle-of-the-day karaoke. But I'd have to turn off my phone and my paycheck writer won't be able to reach me. Either that, or do the loud la-la-la-la I can't hear him routine. Though he may force me into early retirement and I'll be joining Styx singing their stirring anthem "Too much time on my hands." I don't always sing. When I do, I'm usually three sheets to the wind singing soprano and end up losing my voice. Just so you know, this is not how I lost my virginity.

I have found a few more practical ways to occupy my days. Like going to the beach with my lover and best buddies, setting up a shade tent, and playing eight hours of "Aggravation." Sometimes we mix things up by playing "Screw Your Neighbor." You have to rely on cunning in order to insure winning in this competitive world. But mostly, we spend a large part of that time looking for marbles that have fallen into the sand and getting up periodically to take our great galleonic vessels into the seawater so our joints don't stiffen. Yet a word of warning for those doing this during the work week. Stay under a tent as well so you don't walk into your workplace the color of George Hamilton. My boss never knows what shade I am. For all he knows, I look like Edgar Winter. My boss did ask about the background noise of waves and swearing. And although fibbing isn't part of my moral core, I was forced to tell him it was one of those calming sounds of the ocean CD's. But I told him he must have been imagining things when it came to the cursing. Shiftiness is just one of the many services I offer. Other than that, he and I don't feel the need for rapid fire interaction or to keep close tabs on one another.

Someday I will retire from being an office space oddity. I have a well diversified retirement plan of which several dollars are allocated for a jazzy high powered wheelchair with optimal maneuverability, and the rest set aside for Merlot. The body of an average retiree that is usually immobile and grumpy should therefore be a free spirit and filled with fun and fermentation.

Now or Never

I hear it all the time from friends my age. "I just can't do what I used to do." So I decided to challenge myself and go roller skating, and almost ended up in traction. I couldn't just settle for gliding gracefully on wood floors at some roller rink. I had to pick unsmooth asphalt filled with a stretch of patchy potholes. I guess I wanted to bring out my inner child and do something adventurous. I know what you're thinking. My inner nitwit has surfaced and you probably wonder what on God's dangersome earth I will do next. But I've always felt that playfulness fosters good health. Although in this particular case, playfulness resulted in the realignment of my circulatory system.

An apple a day keeps the doctor away. So do probiotics, and keeping ourselves out of harm's way. Okay, there might be more to life than soaring down the street screaming and scaring my neighbors. I'm getting an early start on being an old crash test dummy. I ended up trampling petunias, contoured a row of variegated yucca, and just about took out the Donahue's beagle. But as usual, I got right back up as I have done millions of times in the past when I was down and practically out, and I will do it every time again until doctor's can no longer stitch my broken body back together. But when I take on a blood sport, I must say that every drop of plasma running through my veins feels like I've been adorned with the ichor of an energized Jehovah. At any given moment, we have two choices. Go forward with determination by turning a mission into something not so impossible. Or step back into safety. I'm not about to let grocery shopping or coloring my calendar be the highlight of my day. Yet I do pity the poor souls who might be in my path. There may be other sexagenarians roller skating at the crack of dawn who may likely plow into me. I probably shouldn't be part of the neighborhood watch when I can't see much in dim lighting, nor can I keep my eyes propped open past nine pm.

It's been proven that elders morph into being children again. Although kids are much cuter. I still eat the cream in the middle of an Oreo first. I too get grumpy when I'm tired, don't recall what I did ten minutes ago, have poor impulse control, go to bed early and wake before the rest of civilized society, need someone to explain technology, cry out in frustration, base my entire days around food, babble, and I'm menacing behind the wheel of a car. I also don't have the keenest of eyes or ears. Then there's that attention deficit disorder.

Dum-di-dum…

Sorry for that bit of blankness, but I was trying to remember the other similarities associated with children and older people. Yesterday I was forced to do something I hadn't done since grade school, which was write notes to my boyfriend saying, "I will not yell. I will not misbehave. I will not burn the house to the ground. I will not throw pan lids at the stove when I've scorched something because I walked away and completely forgot that I was cooking something." My man has no use for vandalism, or for sexy looking firefighters blasting water throughout our kitchen. He probably thinks I'm being overdramatic when I'm stressed out. Octopuses eat their arms when they are frazzled. That's way more overdramatic than I'll ever be.

We went to bed last night and I was furiously throwing the blanket back and forth since my stupid body can't decide whether it's hot or cold. Meanwhile my bedmate was looking for the light switch on the lamp. I gave him twenty minutes before I jumped in and showed him how to turn it off. However twenty minutes after that, he had to show me how to shut up when I was still rambling endlessly about the stove incident. I tried to restrain my gustatory gesture of passing gas, something both youngsters and seniors do as well. I told him that my flatulence was all his fault. He should have never taken me to Don Pablo's for dinner. It was a small toot mind you, nothing earth shattering. But every time he says he's going to trade me in for a newer model, I have to remind him that those younger babes have rear end exhaust systems that could also backfire. Since we're such a compromising couple, I said I would light some candles, and he said he would get the fire extinguisher. I was always taught to respect my elders and impress upon them some care and concern. So I randomly switched topics, telling him he should probably wear a helmet when riding his stationary bike. My wisecracking loverboy responded, "And you should shower with your glasses on so you don't use my shampoo and razor by mistake." I wasn't sure whether to clap after that comment, or say Amen.

Before we finally settled into a deep sleep, I expressed another worry about his blood pressure. He told me next time not to leave him waiting at the restaurant table while I went to the restroom for half a century. I explained to him that I spent a distressing twenty minutes of purposeful sobbing in the ladies room, trying to embrace the fact that my wrinkles are worsening. I went on to tell him that when I was young and my mother told me I could grow up to be anything I choose, I didn't exactly choose to be an aging flower child whose petals are wilting. I stayed in the bathroom because I needed a lot more concealer under my eyes, and about twenty other noticeably sad places. I'm just glad age spots and extra weight don't make me more radical with age. But I can tell you this. It's never a good idea to ask a woman in her sixties if she's inconceivably pregnant. She may have just eaten three extra cheesy burritos with a pile of Spanish rice and drank two super-sized margaritas, and topped the night off with a lovely bonfire and eighteen S'Mores.

I have realized that there are three stages of life. Birth, middle age, and what the living hell is this? I am a lot closer to approximating infinity with my higher being than I am going to the kitchen in the morning to freshly baked muffins made by my boyfriend. What I did find were keys still sitting in the lock outside our front entrance. Neither one of us remembers who opened the door and left them there. But at least we remembered enjoying ourselves by getting off our butts and going out to frolic with friends. It's now or never because in this life, there may be no next time or second chances.

Acknowledgements

There are so many people to thank. First and foremost, my three daughters. Without you, I would not have started this ridiculous rant. On the off chance you keep this book on the high priority read list, you will someday realize it's not something that was meant to annoy you. At times we are sure to be misunderstood, you too were put on this earth to achieve your greatest selves. You have enlightened my existence in more ways than I can ever describe. Picture credits go to my beloved Lindsay for your photo genius. Hugs and thanks to Hannah for your validation and babysitting during that fun photo shoot. And gratitude goes to Avril. You have always made me laugh and cheered for me from afar.

It's time to show proper gratitude to my parents. A big fat thanks goes out to them for not believing in birth control.

Special thanks to Nike who emphasized, "Just do it."

To television personality and former stripper Rick Rosner whose intelligence ranges from 140 to 250, depending on the day. He inspired me to look more intellectual by taking Omega 3 fish oil capsules for health, longevity, and to make my brain work better.

To Charlie Chaplin who shares my point of view. "A day without laughter is a day wasted."

Much appreciation to Gustave Flaubert. The *Madame Bovary* writer didn't mince words when he scribed, "Writing is a dog's life, but the only life worth living." I mirrored his tenacious approach to literary originality.

Thanks to my fine fellow writers who taught me how

to cultivate my craft and coerced me to keep on storytelling.

And Joey, Joey, Joey. What else can I say to my graphic designer Joey Seward but thank you, thank you, thank you for your hours of creative expertise and attention to detail.

To my darling publisher and editor Gerri. You didn't chop my book apart and take away my voice like other publishers wanted to do. But we need to discuss that profit margin.

To my delightful and inspirational boyfriend who has given me the space and support to proceed with my dream. You're the best.

Last but not least, to my friends and loyal readers who have appreciated me for exactly who I am.

Patty 💗 xxoo

Dis be my messy desk!

About Patty Clark

My goal in life: To send smiles across America!

Maternal adviser, artiste, proficient hand letterer and calligrapher, cosmo connoisseur, dandelion warrior, and paraprosdokian (before you dash for the dictionary, it means "against expectation"). Empowered by a quirkiness of wit through wisdom when insomnithusiastically writing silly stories.

I reside in northern San Diego County which is somewhere west of Michigan, my home state. Without the inspiration from earth angels in forms of family, friends, and friendly strangers, I would not have kept the crackpot in me alive while penning this ticklish type of hyperbole humor. The only real sense I derive from being alive is the sense of humor.

Idols include other wits: Betty White, Ellen DeGeneres, Erma Bombeck, Jane Lynch, Barney Fife, James Corden, and Paul Lynde.

My biggest supporters: My writers groups and Belly Bandit torso shapewear

Columnist for *The Parson's Sun* newspaper in Kansas, weekend editions, 2013 through 2014

Six-time contest winner with HumorPress.com

Visit my blog: www.damselindismess.com

www.AioniosBooks.com

Made in the USA
Charleston, SC
18 November 2016